The Special Attributes of
The Prophet Muhammad

Ibn Kathir

Al-Firdous Ltd, London
www.al-firdous.co.uk

2001: First Edition

Typeset by Abu Yusuf.

ISBN 1 874263 51 5

Available from: and from

Al-Firdous Ltd.,   Ta-Ha Publishers Ltd.,
10 Fonthill Road   1 Wynne Road
London, N4 3HX   London SW9 0BB

www.al-firdous.co.uk
Email: books@al-firdous.co.uk

Printed in England by
Deluxe Printers, 245-a, Acton Lane,
Park Royal, London NW10 7NR
Tel : 020 8965 1771

Table of Contents

Biography of Ibn Kathir _____ 5

The Prophet's Hajj and 'Umrah _____ 9

The Prophet's Invasions and Missions _____ 10

The Signs of his Prophethood ﷺ _____ 11

Knowledge of Future Happenings and Facts.____ 20

Prophecies About The Prophet ﷺ In The Previous
Divine Books _____ 23

The Prophet's offspring _____ 25

The Prophet's wives _____ 27

The Prophet's Mawali _____ 34

The Prophet's servants _____ 36

Writers of Wahiy (the Revelation) _____ 37

Al-Muadhinun (the Callers for Salat) _____ 38

The Prophet's Camels and Horses_____ 39

The Prophet's Weapons _____ 40

The Prophet's Messengers to Kings of Other Nations
_____ 41

The Visible Features of The Prophet ﷺ_____ 43

The Prophet's Pure Morals _____ 45

The Prophet's Journeys _____ 48

Listening to the Revelation From The Prophet ﷺ_ 54

3

The Number of the Muslims at The Death of The Prophet ﷺ and The Number of Companions Who Transmitted His Traditions _____ *56*

The Attributes of The Prophet ﷺ _____ *58*

The Characteristics that were Specifically Assigned to Him ﷺ but not to Other Prophets. _____ *60*

The Characteristics that were Specifically Assigned to Him ﷺ but not to his Ummah _____ *69*

The Book of Eeman (Faith) _____ 69

The Book of Purification (Taharah) _____ 77

The Book of Salat _____ 82

The Book of Zakat _____ 90

The Book of Siyam (Fasting) _____ 90

The Book of Al-Hajj _____ 92

The Book of Food _____ 93

The Issue of Gifts _____ 96

The Book of Nikah (Marriage) _____ 98
Section 1: What Was Obligatory For Him ﷺ but not on Others _____ 99
Section 2: What Was Prohibited For Him to Marry but not for Others: _____ 100
Section 3: What Was Lawful for Him to Marry but not for Others _____ 101
Section 4: The Virtues Privileged to The Prophet ﷺ and not to Others. _____ 104

The Prophet's Attributes in Jihad _____ *108*

4

Biography of Ibn Kathir

He was Hafiz Abul Fida Ismail ibn Abi Hafs Shihabuddin Omar ibn Kathir ibn Daw ibn Kathir ibn Zar' the Qurasihite - originally from Busra (Syria) - and raised in Damascus. He followed the Shafi'ee school of thought. Ibn Kathir was born in the year 701 (A.H) in an area called Majdal, near Busra, west of Damascus. His father died when he was only four years old and was taken in by his brother and moved to Damascus in 706. Here, he learned from great scholars such as Ibn Asakir, Ishaq ibn Yahya Al-Amudi and the great Ibn Taymiyah who was extremely close to him. He also studied under various other sheikhs who gave him permission in fiqh and Hadith. He made many academic contributions to Islamic sciences. The following are amongst his most prominent:

1. Tafseer of the Qur'an;

2. Al-Bidayah Wannihaya: a history of Muslims from Adam until his (Ibn Kathir's) time;

3. At-Takmeel: a book on the science of Asmaul Rijal (profiles of transmitters of Hadith);

4. Jamiul Masaneed: a book that collects the Hadith from ten major books on Hadith;

5. The classes of Shafi'ee scholars: a list of scholars following the Imam;

6. Extraction of the traditions of Tanbeeh (a Shafi'ee book of jurisprudence);

7. The commentary on al-Bukhari (which he did not finish);

8. The book of laws (again, he did not complete it);

9. The summary to the science of Hadith: a synopsis to the introduction of Ibn Salah's work;

10. Extraction of the traditions to the summary of Ibn Hajib;

11.Musnad of the two sheikhs (Abu Bakr and Umar);

12. Biography of the Prophet ﷺ and

13. The epistle of Jihad.

The author of Manhal says that Ibn Kathir died on Thursday, the 26th of Sha'ban in the year 774 (A.H). May Allah be pleased with him. Ameen.

The Special Attributes of
The Prophet Muhammad

Ibn Kathir

The Prophet's Hajj and 'Umrah

The Prophet's ﷺ last Hajj (pilgrimage) was called the Farewell pilgrimage or the pilgrimage of Islam. Hajj was commanded as an obligation to all Muslims in the year 6 A.H. as stated by some scholars[1], or in the year 9 A.H. by others.

He performed 'Umrah four times. The 'Umrah of Al-Hudaibiyah, which he ﷺ was initially prevented from performing, followed by the 'Umrah of Al-Qada' to fulfil it, then the 'Umrah of Al-Ji'ranah, then the 'Umrah that preceded his Farewell Hajj.

The Prophet ﷺ performed Hajj once before Al-Hijrah (The Emigration to Al-Madinah), and it was said that he ﷺ did Hajj many times, which is the soundest opinion, as he ﷺ used to set out during the Hajj event every year calling people to the Deen (religion) of Allah ﷻ.

---

[1] The Majority of Scholars said that the injunction of Hajj was in the 6th year A.H., giving as proof the time of the verse ﴾And complete the Hajj or 'Umrah in the service of Allah﴿ in the year of Hudaibiyah peace treaty (6 A.H.). However, Ibn Al-Qayyim said in his "Zad Al-Ma'ad" (101/2) that the injunction of Hajj was delayed until the year 9 or 10 and added that it was mentioned by many of our worthy ancestors.

9

The Prophet's Invasions and Missions

Muslim transmitted a Hadith by Abdullah Ibn Buraidah Ibn Al-Husaib Al-Aslami, on the authority of his father, saying: "the Prophet 🕮 made nineteen Ghazwah (Invasions), and fought in eight of them." On the authority of Zaid Ibn Arqam, he said: "the Prophet 🕮 made nineteen Ghazwah, and I attended alongside him 🕮 seventeen of them." As for Muhammad Ibn Ishaq, he said that the Prophet 🕮 was involved in twenty-seven Ghazwah, and his missions totalled thirty-eight. Ibn Hisham mentioned more missions than Ibn Ishaq, and Allah Knows Best.

The Signs of His Prophethood 畿

The scholars have collected more than a thousand miracles regarding the Prophet 畿; here are just some of the Signs of his prophethood 畿:

* The greatest of them all is the Qu'ran Al-Aziz (the powerful), which has no place for falsehood; it is a Revelation from Allah, Full of Wisdom and Worthy of all Praise. Its wondrous nature is in terms of both its form and content:

    The form or language of the Qu'ran is of the highest eloquence and purity; the more knowledge the individual has in this context, the more exaltation he discovers about the Qu'ran. It had defied the eloquent people of its time, known for their fluency of the language, their hostility towards the Qu'ran and their efforts to disprove it; it defied them to produce a similar book, or ten similar Surahs or just one similar Surah, yet they failed and were unable to come out with anything near it. It even defied all Jinn (demons) and Humans to bring forward a similar book, and they failed; Allah 畿 said: ﴾Say: If the whole of mankind and Jinn were to gather together to produce the like of this Qu'ran, they could not produce the like

11

thereof, even if they backed up each other with help and support.$\rangle$[1].

As for its content, it is a mixture of mutual assistance and wisdom, mercy and benefit, the praised outcome and conformity to everything, the attainment of the highest goal and the thwarting of evil and malicious deeds; these are just some of the concepts in the Quran, which are clear to any individual whose mind is void of uncertainty or any heretic tendencies.

Among the signs as well is the fact that the Prophet ﷺ was raised among people who knew his lineage and his upbringing; he was an orphan, trustworthy, truthful, righteous and rightly guided; they all recognised it, except the few who showed obstinacy and arrogance. He ﷺ was illiterate, and did not mingle with cultured people to learn writing and reading. His people never learned anything about the knowledge of the ancestors, until he ﷺ started, at the age of forty, to inform them about ancient nations and events in details. Indeed, most of the Books revealed by Allah ﷻ before the Mission of Prophet ﷺ were subjected to alterations and corruptions, and then the Revelation came to him ﷺ to expose the falsehood in those books and abrogate them all. He ﷺ presented the Right Path to mankind in the most truthful and trustful way, his way of worshipping Allah ﷻ in total

---

[1] Surah Al-Isra', Verse 88.

12

submission, praying to Him ﷻ and displaying great patience with the harm inflicted on him by those who opposed him ﷺ. He ﷺ showed the most distinguished moral qualities: generosity, courage, righteousness, decency, and others that have never been assembled in a person before or since.

All the information and knowledge he ﷺ imparted as they are recorded in the Qur'an and his traditions ﷺ, and all the future events and facts that happened just as he had predicted.

- Allah ﷻ displayed some unusual phenomena at the hands of His Prophet ﷺ such as: the cleaving of the moon as Allah ﷻ said in Surat Al-Qamar. One night the polytheists demanded a sign of prophethood from the Messenger of Allah ﷺ; he obliged and pointed to the moon, which split in two in response to his request ﷺ. The polytheists, thinking that the prophet ﷺ might have bewitched them, asked some people in the surroundings if they had seen anything unusual, and they also reported the cleaving of the moon. And this account was successively related by the scholars and was transmitted by a number of Companions ﷺ[1].

- Among the signs of his prophethood: the blessings from his supplications to Allah ﷻ. Al-Hafidh Abu

---

[1] Transmitted by Al-Bukhari (3636) and Muslim (2800), on the authority of Abdullah Ibn Mas'ud ﷺ; other authorities include: Anas, Ibn 'Abbas, Ali, Hudhaifah, Jubair Ibn Mat'am, Ibn Omar.

Bakr Al-Baihaqi managed to compile most of them in his book "Dala'il Annubuwah" (The Signs of Prophethood), and these are some of them: the Prophet ﷺ approached the lamb that was in the care of Ibn Mas'ud ﷺ, invoked Allah ﷻ for a blessing, and after reciting the Name of Allah, he started milking its newly full udders; he ﷺ drank its milk and offered some to Abu Bakr[2]. A similar sign took place with the goat of Ummu Ma'bad[1].

- The Prophet ﷺ prayed for Attufail Ibn 'Amru, who consequently had a blessed sign on the side of his whip and a light in his face seen from afar[2]. The Prophet ﷺ made similar supplications to grant two other companions (Usaid Ibn Al-Hudair and 'Abbad Ibn Bishr Al-Ansari) blessings from Allah ﷻ.

- The Prophet ﷺ prayed against the seven who sneered at him as he was performing Salat, and they were duly killed in Badr[3]. He ﷺ also invoked Allah's wrath on the son of Abu Lahab, and Allah responded positively to his Messenger's

---

[2] Transmitted by Ahmed (462, 379/1), Attayalisi (353) and Abu Ya'la (4985), on the authority of Abdullah Ibn Mas'ud. Sheikh Shakir (May Allah's Mercy be upon him) authenticated the chain of this hadith.

[1] Transmitted by Al-Hakim (10-9/3), Adhahabi agreed on its authenticity, and was also transmitted by Attabarani in 'Al-Kabeer'(3605).

[2] Transmitted by Ibn Ishaq in 'As-Seerah' (33/2)

[3] Transmitted by Al-Bukhari (240) and Muslim (1794), on the authority of Abdullah Ibn Mas'ud ﷺ.

14

supplications by setting a lion on him while on a journey to Syria[4].

- The Prophet ﷺ, in an incident on his migration to Al-Madinah, invoked Allah against the rider Suraqah and immediately his horse's legs sank into the ground, then he ﷺ prayed for their release and Allah ﷻ released them[1].

- Many of the Prophet's blessings occurred when the Muslims were engaged in battles against the enemies of Islam:

  ◆ In the battles of Badr and Hunain, the Prophet ﷺ threw a handful of pebbles at his enemies and hit every one of them.

  ◆ During the Battle of Badr, he ﷺ handed 'Akkashah a stump which turned into a sharp sword[2].

  ◆ In the Battle of Uhud, the Prophet ﷺ replaced the eye of Qatadah Ibn Annu'man Adhafari

---

[4] It is 'Utbah Ibn Abi Lahab, and the Hadith was transmitted by Abu Nu'aim in (Addala'il) (380).
[1] Transmitted by Al-Bukhari (3615) and Muslim (2009), on the authority of Al-Barra' quoting Abu Bakr ﷺ
[2] Transmitted by Ibn Saad in 'Attabaqat' (125/1), it has a weak chain and it is Mursal (Chain of authorities does not go back further than the 2nd generation after the Prophet ﷺ). Also transmitted by Ibn Ishaq in 'Seerah' (202/2) with no mention of its chain of authorities.

15

after it had fallen out onto his cheek[3], and it was thereafter undistinguishable from the other.

- The Prophet ﷺ was able to know some hidden news with the help of Allah ﷻ. He ﷺ informed Al-'Abbas, who was captive at the time, of the money he and his wife – Ummu Al-Fadl – had hidden at their doorsteps, and Al-'Abbas ؓ confirmed it[1]. He ﷺ also informed 'Umair Ibn Wahab of his intention to kill the Prophet ﷺ while pretending to bring the ransom for the prisoners of Badr. 'Umair ؓ admitted his intentions and embraced Islam thereupon[2].

- On the day of Al-Khandaq battle, the Prophet ﷺ fed his huge army of nearly a thousand warriors with only one lamb, and a portion of barleycorn as provisions in the house of Jaber[3], along a with few

---

[3] A sound Hadith, transmitted by Abu Nu'aim in 'Addala'il' (416), on the authority of Qatadah. Transmitted by Abu Ya'laa (1549), and Al-Haithami said in 'Azzawa'id' collection (298/8): the chain of authority mentioned by Abu Ya'laa includes Yahya Ibn Abdelhamid Al-Hamani, who is considered weak. The hadith was also transmitted by Attabarani in 'Al-Kabeer'.
[1] A sound Hadith, transmitted by Ahmed (353/1) on the authority of Ibn 'Abbas. Al-Haithami said in his collection (85-86/6): it include an unnamed authority but the rest of the authorities are trustworthy. Al-Hafidh said in 'Al-Fath' that the Hadith has a sound chain.
[2] A sound Hadith, transmitted by Abu Nu'aim in 'Addala'il' (413), on the authority of 'Urwah Ibn Az-Zubair, and it is Mursal.
[3] Transmitted by Al-Bukhari (4101) and Muslim (2039), on the authority of Jaber Ibn Abdellah ؓ.

dates brought over by the daughter of Bashir[4]. He 襤 also fed around eighty people with a meal nearly concealed by his blessed hands[5], and did a similar thing on the day he 襤 married Zainab, daughter of Jahsh[1]. And on the day of Tabuk, the Prophet's blessings were extraordinary; he 襤 was able to provide food for his huge army, and each of them managed to fill his provision bag with cooked meat from one single goat[2]. The Prophet 襤 gave Abu Hurairah 襤 a leather bag of food that he used to provide for himself all his life, he 襤 gave many supplies from it for the path of Allah 襤. The supply bag was still in his position until the days of the killing of 'Uthman 襤[3].

- The Prophet 襤 made supplications to Allah 襤 when the Muslims were suffering from a drought and it was a day where there was no sight of a cloud in the sky. He 襤 was still at the pulpit in the mosque praying when water started dripping on his

---

[4] Transmitted by Ibn Ishaq in 'Seerah' (108/3) and Al-Baihaqi in 'Addala'il' (427/3), on the authority of the daughter of Bashir Ibn Saad, sister of Annu'man Ibn Bashir.
[5] Transmitted by Al-Bukhari (5381) and Muslim (2040), on the authority of Anas Ibn Malik 襤.
[1] Transmitted by Muslim (1428), on the authority of Anas Ibn Malik. It was also transmitted by Attirmidi (3218) and An-nasa'I (3386).
[2] Transmitted by Al-Bukhari (2484) and Muslim (1729) on the authority of Salamah Ibn Al-Akwa' 襤.
[3] Transmitted by Attirmidi (3839), Ahmed (352/2)and Abu An-Nu'aim in 'Addala'il' (341), on the authority of Abu Hurairah 襤. Also mentioned by Sheikh Al-Albani in Sahih Attirmidi (3015).

beard from the ceiling of the mosque. The clouds covered the sky of Al-Madina and obscured every clear spot[1].

- The Prophet ﷺ prayed against Quraish and Allah ﷻ inflicted His stern punishment of strain and extreme tension on them, to the extent that they begged the Prophet ﷺ for mercy; he ﷺ sympathized with them and Allah ﷻ lifted his punishment[2].

- In another event, the Prophet ﷺ was preparing to do wudu' (ritual ablution before Salat) using a container with very little water, when he ﷺ was approached by some people who expressed their wish to perform wudu' with him ﷺ. He ﷺ inserted his blessed hand in the container and invoked Allah ﷻ for His blessings; consequently, water flowed out from between his fingers ﷺ[3]. A similar Sign took place on the day of Al-Hudaibiyah, and the army numbered one thousand four hundred. Jaber said: 'It would have been enough for us even if we had been a hundred thousand.'[1] The companions of the Prophet used to witness many instances of this particular water Sign in his journeys ﷺ. Jabber

---

[1] Transmitted by Al-Bukhari (1013) and Muslim (897) on the authority of Anas Ibn Malik ﷻ.
[2] Transmitted by Al-Bukhari (1007) and Muslim (2798) on the authority of Abdullah Ibn Mas'ud ﷻ.
[3] Transmitted by Al-Bukhari (169) and Muslim (2279) on the authority of Anas Ibn Malik ﷻ.
[1] Transmitted by Al-Bukhari (3576) and Muslim (1856) on the authority of Jaber Ibn Abdellah ﷻ.

added: 'When the Prophet ﷺ ordered me to pour a drop of water in the container, I feared the dry bottom of the pot would absorb it; the Messenger of Allah put his hand inside and invoked Allah ﷻ, then immediately water sprang from between his fingers for his companions to drink and do wudu'[2].

---

[2] Transmitted by Muslim (3013) on the authority of Jaber Ibn Abdellah ﷺ.

Knowledge of Future Happenings and Facts.

The Prophet ﷺ informed his Ummah about future events, as they were revealed by Allah ﷻ in the Qu'ran: The prevailing of His religion, the exalting of the word of Allah ﷻ and the succession on earth of those in his Ummah, who believed in Allah, and his Messenger and did good deeds.

He ﷺ reported that the Romans would conquer the Persians for a number of years[1].

He ﷺ informed his people, who were at the outskirts of Makkah, that Allah ﷻ Had set termite on a collection of papers, that had been placed on top of Al-Ka'bah by Quraish, and which included an agreement by Quraish to boycott Bani Hashim. The termite ate everything except the reference to Allah ﷻ[2].

---

[1] An Authentic Hadith transmitted by Attirmidi (3193) Ahmed (276, 304/1) and Al-Hakim (410/2), on the authority of Abdullah Ibn 'Abbas ﷺ.
[2] Transmitted by Abu Nu'aim in 'Addala'il' (205), on the authority of 'Urwah, and it is Mursal. It has a weak chain. Also transmitted by Al-Baihaqi in 'Addala'il' (311/2) on the authority of Az-Zuhari. Also see Zad Al-Ma'ad (29/3).

He ﷺ fortold before the Battle of Badr each of the spots where soldiers would die, and it happened exactly as he ﷺ described it[3].

He ﷺ prophesied that the wealth of Khosrau (the Persian King) and Caesar would be spent in the cause of Allah ﷻ[4], and informed his Ummah that their reign would spread far over the earth[5].

He ﷺ prophesied that the Hour (Day of Judgment) would not come until the Muslim Ummah had fought a nation whose people are described as having small eyes and chiseled noses in wide bulged faces as if they are shielded[1]; and that was the case of the Tatars.

He ﷺ foretold the fighting of 'Ali ؓ against Al-Khawarij – the dissenters who rebelled against the caliphate of 'Ali ؓ[2].

He ﷺ predicted that Al-Hasan Ibn 'Ali ؓ would be the man that Allah ﷻ would choose to reconcile two great Muslim parties[3].

---

[3] Transmitted by Muslim (1779) and Abu Dawud (2681), on the authority of Anas Ibn Malik ؓ.
[4] Transmitted by Al-Bukhari (3618) and Muslim (2918), on the authority of Abu Hurairah ؓ.
[5] Transmitted by Muslim (2889) Abu Dawud (4252) and Attirmidi (2176), on the authority of Thawban ؓ.
[1] Transmitted by Al-Bukhari (2929) and Muslim (2912), on the authority of Abu Hurairah. ؓ.
[2] Transmitted by Al-Bukhari (3344) and Muslim (1064), on the authority of Abu Saeed Al-Khudri ؓ.

21

He ﷺ prophesied that 'Ammar would be killed by the unjust party[4]; and he was indeed killed in the battle of Siffeen with 'Ali ؓ

He ﷺ foretold of the emergence of a fire in the land of Al-Hijaz (Arabian Peninsula) whose light would be reflected on the neck of camels in Basra[5]; indeed, this event took place in the 650s A.H.

---

[3] Transmitted by Al-Bukhari (2704), on the authority of Abu Bikrah ؓ.
[4] Transmitted by Al-Bukhari (447) and Muslim (2915).
[5] Transmitted by Al-Bukhari (7118) and Muslim (2902), on the authority of Abu Hurairah ؓ.

Prophecies About The Prophet ﷺ In The Previous Divine Books

In the Torah and the Injeel (Bible), Allah ﷻ foretold the appearance of the Prophet ﷺ. Likewise, He ﷻ Told us in the Quran of the words the Prophet Issa (Jesus) عليه السلام said to the Children of Israel referring to the Prophet Muhammad ﷺ: ﴿and giving glad tidings of a Messenger to come after me, whose name shall be Ahmad﴾. Al-Bukhari[1] transmitted on the authority of Abdullah Ibn 'Amru that the characteristics of the Prophet ﷺ were described in the Torah.

In the existing Torah, whose authenticity is assumed by the Jews, the first Book says that Allah ﷻ revealed Himself to Ibrahim (Abraham) عليه السلام, and said to him "Travel along the length and breadth of the earth as a glorification to your son" However, none was given the right to rule the whole world but Muhammad ﷺ, as it is mentioned in the Sahih traditions; he ﷺ said: "Allah drew the ends of the world together for my

---

[1] Transmitted by Al-Bukhari (2125) on the authority of 'Ata' Ibn Yasar who said: I met Abdullah Ibn 'Amru Ibn Al-'As ؓ and I said to him: 'Tell me about the attributes of the Prophet ﷺ as described in the Torah', he said: Yes, by Allah ! he is described in the Torah with some of his attributes in the Quran: "O Prophet! We have truly sent you as a witness, as a bringer of glad tidings and as a warner, and a protector to the illiterate. You are my Slave and my Messenger, I called you the Reliant, and you are neither harsh nor crude nor boisterous in the markets."

sake. I have seen its eastern and western ends. The dominion of my Ummah will reach those ends, which have been drawn together near me"[1]. In the first book of the Torah also, Allah ﷻ promised Ibrahim that his son Isma'el (Ishmael) عليه السلام would have a strong hold over all nations; they would all be under his reign, including those of his brothers[1]. However, the People of the Book knew that Isma'el عليه السلام never entered Syria and that his brothers were never under his reign; instead, that was left to his son – in lineage – Muhammad ﷺ. None of the Arabs ever conquered Egypt and Syria before the Ummah of Muhammad ﷺ, but these were conquered during the caliphate of As-Siddiq (Abu Bakr) and Al-Faruq (Omar) رضي الله عنهما.

In Book four of the existing Torah, there is a verse which says: ﴿A prophet was set for them from their close relations, and brothers like you Musa (Moses), and I will put my word in his mouth.﴾ It is clear to them and to everyone that Allah ﷻ did not send a prophet from the offspring of Isma'el except Muhammad ﷺ. In fact, there was no prophet from the Children of Isra'el similar to Musa عليه السلام except 'Issa عليه السلام, but the Jews do not accept his prophethood, and he is not the offspring of their brothers; instead, he is related to them through his mother, therefore, the meaning of the above verse focuses on Prophet Muhammad ﷺ.

---

[1] Transmitted by Muslim (2889) Abu Dawud (4252) and Attirmidi, on the authority of Thawban رضي الله عنه.
[1] See Genesis 21 verse 18.

24

The Prophet's Offspring

The Prophet 🌺 had all his children by Khadijah 🌺, daughter of Khuwailid, except Ibrahim, who was born from Mariyah Al-Kubtiyah.

They are:
Al-Qasim, after whom the Prophet 🌺 was surnamed (Abu Al-Qasim) because he was the eldest of his children, then Zainab, then Ruqayah, then Ummu Kalthum, then Fatimah.

After the Revelation of the message, his son Abdullah was born, he used to be called At-Tayyib (the good) and At-Tahir (the pure), because he was born in the Islamic era. It was said that he was called At-Tahir without At-Tayyib, and this was authenticated by some scholars. Then Ibrahim was born of Mariyah in Al-Madinah in the year 8A.H. He died aged one year and ten months, and for this reason the Prophet 🌺 said: "He certainly has a foster mother in Paradise."[1]

They all died before him 🌺, apart from Fatimah 🌺; she died six months later and this is the widely known narration. Other accounts claim her death was eight months, or seventy days, or three months, or a hundred days after the Prophet 🌺 had passed away. Ali 🌺 performed Salat for her funeral, and it was said in a

---

[1] transmitted by Al-Bukhari (1382) on the authority of Al-Barra' Ibn 'Azib, and Muslim (2316), on the authority of Anas Ibn Malik 🌺.

strange (Gharib) account that it was Abu Bakr. The people who were in charge to wash her were: Ali, Al'Abbas, Asma' Bintu 'Amees – As-Siddiq's wife – and Salmah Ummu Rafi' who was her midwife[2].

---

[2] Transmitted by Ashafi'I, Abu Nu'aim, Addaraqutni and Al-Hakim, and it has a sound chain of authorities.

The Prophet's Wives

Khadeejah, daughter of Khuwailid, was the first woman he ﷺ married while in Makkah. She was the first person of trust when he ﷺ was honoured with the Revelation, and she was authentically the first person to believe in his Message. Another account said that Abu Bakr was the first to believe in him, but this is considered unusual. He ﷺ did not marry another woman while Khadijah was still alive because of her great and dear position in his life ﷺ. There were diverse opinions as to who was dearer to him ﷺ: Khadijah or 'Aisha ﷺ. A group of scholars thought that the Prophet's high esteem and preference was to Khadijah ﷺ first, she died a year and a half before Al-Hijrah (Migration).

He ﷺ married Sawdah Bintu Zam'ah, Al-Qurashiyah Al-'Amiriyah, after the death of Khadijah ﷺ in Makkah, and when she was older, he ﷺ wanted to divorce her, but she reconciled him and offered her day (the time the Prophet ﷺ spent at her place) to 'Aisha ﷺ. He ﷺ accepted and it was regarding this case that Allah ﷺ revealed: ❨And if a woman fears cruelty or aversion on her husband's part, there is no sin on them both if they make terms of peace between themselves❩[1]. She ﷺ died in the last days of the Emir of the Believers 'Omar Ibn Al-Khattab ﷺ.

---

[1] Surah An-Nissa', Verse 128.

It was said that the Prophet ﷺ married 'Aisha before Sawdah, but he did not consummate the marriage until the month of Shawal in the year 2 A.H.. She was the only virgin he ﷺ married and he ﷺ loved her more than any other woman. She had many distinguished qualities and glorious deeds that were mentioned in the Quran and the Sunnah (traditions) of the Prophet ﷺ, and no woman in our Ummah was known to have reached the level of knowledge that 'Aisha had. She was the most learned and she ﵂ died in year 58 A.H.

The Prophet ﷺ married Hafsah, daughter of 'Omar Ibn Al-Khattab ﵂; in the year 13 A.H., he ﷺ divorced her then remarried her ﵂. She died in the year 41 A.H. and it was said she ﵂ died in the year 45 or 50 A.H.

The Prophet ﷺ married Ummu Salamah – her name was Hind Bintu Abi Umayah the Quraishi – after the death of her husband Abi Salamah 'Abdullah Ibn Abd Al-Asad Ibn Hilal Ibn Abdullah Ibn Makhzum in the aftermath of the Battle of Badr. Then, when the period of Iddat (the legally prescribed period of waiting during which a woman may not remarry after being divorced) ended, the Prophet ﷺ married her at the beginning of the 3rd year A.H. The man who was in charge of formulating her act of marriage was her son Omar as it was transmitted by An-Nassa'i following the chain of authorities that include: Hamad Ibn Salamah, Thabit Al-Bunaniy, Ibn Omar Ibn Abi Salamah, his father and finally Um Salamah. The author, Muhammad Al-Halabi has gathered a special volume for these issues, where he explained that the

28

Omar mentioned in this Hadith is indeed Omar Ibn Al-Khattab ﷺ, because he was the man who contracted her engagement to the Messenger of Allah ﷺ; however, Al-Waqidi reported that her legal guardian was her son, and that is the authentic account, Allah Willing. It was also mentioned that the Prophet ﷺ married her without the presence of her legal guardian, and Allah Knows Best.

Al-Waqidi said that Umm Salamah died in year 59 A.H., and others said she passed away during the caliphate of Yazeed Ibn Mu'awiyah in year 62 A.H.

The Prophet ﷺ married Zainab Bintu Jahsh in the month of Dhel-Qi'dah, in year 5 A.H.; and on the morning of the wedding day, the Divine Injunction of Hijab was revealed to the Prophet ﷺ. Anas Ibn Malik, the Prophet's servant and the authority of this Hadith, said that he was prevented from entering the premises of the Prophet's wives from that particular day, because he was fifteen by then[1]. And Allah Knows Best.

Her legal guardian and protector was Allah ﷻ, He said: ⟪So when Zaid had accomplished his desire from her (i.e. divorced her), We gave her to you in marriage⟫[2]. Al-Bukhari transmitted that she used to boast before the Prophet's other wives of the fact they were married by their relatives and she was married by Allah ﷻ's

---

[1] Transmitted by Al-Bukhari (4791) and Muslim (1428), on the authority of Anas Ibn Malik ﷺ.
[2] Surah Al-Ahzab, Verse 37.

29

command in the sky. She was the first among the Prophet's wives to die; Al-Waqidi said she died in year 20 A.H. and Omar Ibn Al-Khattab 🕌 performed salat for her.

The Prophet 🕌 married Juwairiyah Bintu Al-Harith Ibn Abu Dirar on the day he 🕌 invaded her people in the Water place called Al-Muraisi' in year 6 A.H., she was captured (as a booty) by Thabit Ibn Qais Ibn Shammas who demanded a ransom if she wanted to be freed. She came to the Prophet 🕌 asking for his help, he 🕌 paid the ransom, set her free and married her. She 🕌 died in the year 50 A.H., although according to Al-Waqidi she died in the year 56 A.H.

The Prophet 🕌 married Safiyah Bintu Huyai Ibn Akhtab, the Jewish woman from Bani An-Nadeer, when he 🕌 chose her from the women spoils taken at the battle of Khaibar. The Prophet 🕌 set her free and made it her dowry for the marriage, which took place in the year 7 A.H. He consummated the marriage with her on their way back to Al-Madinah, and covered her; it was then the companions knew that she had become one of the Mothers of the Believers. Al-Waqidi said that she died in the year 50 A.H.; others said in the year 36 A.H. and Allah Knows Best.

The Prophet 🕌 married Um Habibah, Ramlah Bintu Abu Sufyan Sakhr Ibn Harb Ibn Umayah Ibn Abd Shams, while she was in Al-Habasha (Ethiopia) after the death of her husband 'Ubaidullah Ibn Jahsh. The Prophet 🕌 sent 'Amru Ibn Umayah Ad-Damri to

30

contract the marriage and bring her to Al-Madinah. An-Najashi, the King of Al-Habasha, accepted the Prophet's request and even offered her four hundred dinars as dowry on his behalf. She 🌸 died in the year 44 A.H. according to Abu 'Ubaid, as for Abu Bakr Ibn Abi Khaithamah, he said she 🌸 died in the year 59 A.H. a year before the death of her brother Mu'awiyah.

The Prophet 🌸 married Maimunah, the daughter of Al-Harith, in the month of Dhul-Qa'dah in the 7th year A.H. There were different opinions as to whether he 🌸 was in a state of Ihram or not. Ibn 'Abbas in a Hadith Sahih[1] said the Prophet 🌸 was in Ihram; and some scholars said it was one of his characteristics, following a Hadith transmitted by Muslim on the authority of 'Uthman that the Prophet 🌸 said: 'the Muslim in a state of Ihram does not marry or get engaged.'[2] However, it was said that he 🌸 was not in a state of Ihram, as transmitted by Muslim[3] on the authority of Maimunah who said that the Prophet 🌸 married her and consummated marriage with her while in a halal state (not in a state of Ihram to perform Al-Hajj). The majority of scholars have considered this Hadith ahead of Hadith Ibn 'Abbas, because Maimunah is the one concerned in the story, and it was similarly accounted for by Abu Rafi' in a narration by

---

[1] Transmitted by Al-Bukhari (5114) and Muslim (1410).
[2] Transmitted by Muslim (1409) Abu Dawud (1841) and Attirmidi (840), on the authority of 'Uthman 🌸.
[3] Transmitted by Muslim (1411) Abu Dawud (1843) and Attirmidi (845), on the authority of Maimunah Bintu Al-Harith 🌸.

Attirmidi on his authority[1]; he was the mediator between them. She died in the place where the Prophet ﷺ consummated with her after the Compensatory Pilgrimage in year 51 A.H. and 'Abdullah Ibn 'Abbas ؓ, her sister's son, performed Salat at her funeral.

Those were the nine wives, after Khadeejah as it is described in the two Sahih Books, whom the Prophet ﷺ had left behind, and in another narration in the Sahih, the Prophet ﷺ died and left behind eleven of his wives; however, the first account is the authentic one.

Qatadah Ibn Du'amah said: the Prophet ﷺ married fifteen wives, consummated the marriage with thirteen, lived with eleven and died and left behind nine. Al-Hafidh Abu Abdullah Muhammad Ibn Abd Al-Wahid Al-Maqdisi made a similar narration on the authority of Anas ؓ in his book 'Al-Mukhtarah'; this is the widely known account.

Besides these, the Prophet ﷺ had two concubines. The first was Mariyah Bintu Sham'un the Coptic, Umm Ibraheem the son of the Prophet ﷺ. She was a present from Al-Muqawqis, the commander of Alexandria and Egypt, along with her sister Shereen, a horse named Mabur and a mare named Adduldul. The Prophet ﷺ offered Shereen to Hassan Ibn Thabit and she gave birth to their son Abderahman. Mariyah died in the month of Muharram in year 16 A.H. and it was Omar

---

[1] A Weak Hadith transmitted by Attirmidi (841) Addarami (38/2) and Ahmed (392-393/6). And Sheikh Al-Albani said in 'Erwa' Al-Ghalil' (1849): the Hadith is weak.

Ibn Al-Khattab ﷺ who assembled people for her funeral, performed Salat for her and buried her in Al-Baqee'ﷺ. As for the second concubine, she was Raihanah Bintu 'Amru, and it was said Bintu Zaid, he ﷺ chose her among the captives from Bani Quraidha, and he ﷺ later set her free to join her people.

The Prophet's Mawali[1]

The names of all dependants who were at the service of the Prophet ﷺ were listed alphabetically by Al-Hafidh Al-Kabeer Abu Al-Qasim Ibn 'Asakir at the beginning of his History book; they are: Ahmar, named Abu 'Usaib; Aswad; Aflah; Anas; Ayman Ibn Um Ayman; Badham; Thawban Ibn Bujdud; Dhakwan; Rafi'; Ruwaifi'; Zaid Ibn Haritha; Zaid the grandfather of Hilal Ibn Yasar; Sabiq; Salim; Sa'eed; Safeenah; Salman Al-Farisi; Sulaim, named Abu Kabshah and mentioned among those present at the Battle of Badr; Saleh; Dumairah; 'Ubaidullah Ibn Aslam; 'Ubaid; Abu Safiyah; Fudalah Al-Yamaani; Qusair; Kirkirah; Mabur the Quptic; Mud'im; Maimun; Nafi'; Nabeel; Hurmuz; Hisham; Waqid; Wardan; Yasar; Abu Uthailah; Abu Bikrah; Abu Al-Hamra'; Abu Rafi'; and Abu 'Ubaid.

Abu Zakariyah An-Nawawiy also assembled all the names of the Prophet's servants in his book "Tahdhib Al-Asma' wa Al-Lughat".

As for his bondmaids, they were: Umaimah; Birkah-Um Ayman; Khadrah; Ridwah; Raihanaah; Salamah-

---

[1] the plural of Mawla, a person with whom a tie of wala' (the tie of clientage established between a freed slave and the person who frees him, whereby the freed slave becomes integrated into the family of that person) has been established, usually by having been a slave and then set free.

34

Um Rafi'; Shereen; Mariyah- mother of his son Ibraheem ﷺ; Maimunah Bintu Saad; Um Dumairah; and Um 'Ayyash. Abu Zakariyah – May Allah Have Mercy on him – said that the Prophet ﷺ did not possess all these maids at the same time but rather in separate periods of his life ﷺ.

The Prophet's Servants

A group of the Prophet's companions committed themselves willingly to serve the Prophet ﷺ:

Abdullah Ibn Mas'ud was looking after the Prophet's shoes; he would help the Prophet put them on whenever he ﷺ stood up to leave, and would keep hold of them in his hand when he ﷺ sat down.

Al-Mugheerah Ibn Shu'bah was the guard to protect him ﷺ.
'Uqbah Ibn 'Amir was in charge of the Prophet's mare, he ﷺ used to guide and lead the mare in the Prophet's ﷺ journeys.

There were also other Companions at the service of the Prophet ﷺ i.e.: Anas Ibn Malik, Rabee'ah Ibn Kaab, Bilal and Dhu Makhbar, the nephew of An-Najashi the King of Al-Habashah.

Writers of Wahiy (the Revelation)

The Writers of the Revelation as listed by Al-Hafidh Abu Al-Qasim in his book are as follows:

Abu Bakr, Omar, 'Uthman, 'Ali, Az-Zubair, Ubai Ibn Ka'b, Zaid Ibn Thabit, Mu'awiyah Ibn Abi Sufyan, Muhammad Ibn Abi Salamah, Al-Arqam Ibn Abi Al-Arqam, Aban Ibn Sa'eed Ibn Al-'As, his brother Khalid, Thabit Ibn Qais, Handhalah Ibn Ar-Rabi' Al-Usaidi, Khalid Ibn Al-Waleed, Abdullah Ibn Al-Arqam, Abdullah Ibn Zadi Ibn Abdi-Rabih, Al-'Ala' Ibn 'Utbah, Al-Mugheerah Ibn Shu'bah, and Sharhabeel Ibn Hasanah.

Al-Muadhinun (the Callers for Salat)

The Prophet ﷺ had four *muadhins*; there were two in Al-Madinah: Bilal Ibn Rabah and 'Amru Ibn Umm Maktum, the blind, and it was said his name was Abdullah ﷺ.

Saad Al-Quradh ﷺ was the Muadhin in Quba', and Abu Mahdurah was in Makkah ﷺ.

The Prophet's Camels and Horses

The Prophet ﷺ had three camels: Al-'Adba', Al-Jid'a' and Al-Qaswa'.

An-Nawawi reported that Muhammad Ibn Ibraheem Attaimi said that the Prophet ﷺ had only one camel, which had these three descriptive names, but this narration is an exception.

As for his horses, he ﷺ had a horse named 'Assakb', which he ﷺ used for his first invasion.

He ﷺ had a horse named 'Sabhah', which he ﷺ used in a race, and another one named 'Al-Murtajiz', which he ﷺ bought from a Bedouin in the presence of Khazeemah Ibn Thabit ﷺ.

Sahl Ibn Saad said the Prophet ﷺ had three other horses: 'Lizar', 'Adharib' and 'Al-Lukhaif'; this made six in total, and a seventh was 'Al-Wird', a gift from Tamim Ad-Dariy.

The Prophet ﷺ had a mare called Al-Duldul, a gift from Al-Muqawqis; he ﷺ went to the Battle of Hunain riding it. It lived on after the death of the Prophet ﷺ, and was left in the care of Ali and later in the care of Abdullah Ibn Ja'far ﷺ.

Also in the possession of the Prophet ﷺ was a donkey called 'Ufair and some cattle.

The Prophet's Weapons

The Prophet ﷺ had three lances, three bows, six swords including Dhu Al-Faqqar, which he ﷺ gained in Badr, Tirs and Dir'.

He ﷺ also had a ring, a big wooden container, a black squared flag and a white banner – although it is also said the banner was black.

The Prophet's Messengers to Kings of Other Nations

The Prophet ﷺ sent many messengers to leaders of other nations calling them to Islam:

He ﷺ sent 'Amru Ibn Umayah Ad-Damri with a letter to An-Najashiy who embraced Islam ﷺ.

He ﷺ also sent Dihiyah Ibn Khaleefa Al-Kalbiy to Heraclius, the great emperor of Rome, who is said to have shown an interest in Islam but never embraced it. Some scholars said he died a Muslim and Sunaid Ibn Dawud transmitted in his Tafseer a Hadith mursal that indicates the conversion to Islam of Heraclius. However, Abu 'Ubaid transmitted in his book 'Al-Amwal' a hadith mursal, which confirmed that the Roman king had never embraced Islam[1].

Abdullah Ibn Hudhafah Assahmiy was sent to Khosrau, the Persian King, who arrogantly tore up the Prophet's letter and defiantly refused to accept anything from him. The Prophet ﷺ cursed him and Allah ﷻ destroyed him and his kingdom.

---

[1] Ibn Hibban transmitted in his Sahih book (1628), on the authority of Anas Ibn Malik ﷺ, he said: the Prophet ﷺ said: 'Who would take my book hereby to Heraclius and get granted Paradise?', this is a very long Hadith, in the end of which, the Prophet ﷺ said od Heraclius: 'The enemy of Allah lied, he is not a Muslim, he is still embracing Christianity.'

Haatib Ibn Balta'ah was sent to Al-Muqawqis, the king of Alexandria and Egypt, who showed friendship to Muslims and exchanged presents with the Prophet ﷺ, but was never known to have embraced Islam.

'Amru Ibn Al-'As was sent to the two kings of 'Oman who embraced Islam.

Sulait Ibn 'Amru Al-'Amiri was sent to Hawdha Ibn Ali Al-Hanafi in Al-Yamamah.

Shuja' Ibn Wahb Al-Asadiy was sent to Al-Harith Ibn Abi Shamar Al-Ghassaniy, the king of Al-Balqa' in Syria.

Al-Muhajir Ibn Abi Umayah Al-Makhzumiy was sent to Al-Harith Al-Himyari.

Al-'Ala' Ibn Al-Hadramiy was sent to Al-Mundir Ibn Sawaa Al-'Abdiy, the king of Bahrain, who embraced Islam.

Abu Musa Al-Ash'ari and Mu'adh Ibn Jabal were sent to the people of Yemen, who all embraced Islam.

The Visible Features of The Prophet ﷺ

The scholars have classified his features in one volume, and the best to have compiled them was Al-Imam Abu 'Issa Muhammad Ibn 'Issa Ibn Sawrah Attirmidhi, may Allah Have Mercy on him, in his book "Ashama'il". Al-Hafidh Abu Al-Qasim Ibn 'Asakir and Al-Imam Al-Hafidh Abu Al-Hajjaj Al-Mizziy edited an extended discussion of the subject in a book called "Tahdheeb Al-Kamal".

Al-Imam An-Nawawi said in his abridged chapter: the Prophet ﷺ was neither excessively tall nor extremely small, he was neither white nor brown, and his hair was neither curly nor lanky.

When he ﷺ died, there were no more than twenty grey hairs in his head, his hair was shoulder length, and at times was down to his earlobes, his beard was thick and so were his fingers and toes; overall, he was in good condition physically. His face ﷺ was fairly round, his head was large and his joints were rather big. He ﷺ had big black eyes with long eyebrows, and had thin hair extending from his chest down to his navel. He ﷺ used to walk at a good pace but always looked at ease, and it seemed as if the earth had folded itself up to shorten the distance for him. His face would shine, as it was moon-like, his voice was sound, his cheeks were plain, his mouth was large. The Seal of Prophethood, which was similar in size to a pigeon's egg, was between his shoulders.

His hair used to hang loose, and he would part it; he used to comb his beard and would apply kuhul to his eyes three times before he went to bed.

His favourite clothing was al-qamees (shirt) and al-hibrah, a sort of wrap covering garment, in white; the sleeves of his qamees were to his wrist. He ﷺ once wore red clothing; he also wore a wrap-around cloak or a loose outer garment as cover. He ﷺ once combined two green piece of clothing, and another time he ﷺ had a black 'imamah (turban) the sides of which were laid on his shoulder. He ﷺ wore a ring, wore socks and sandals or shoes.

Anas Ibn Malik said: 'I have never touched silk or a silky garment softer than the palm of the Prophet's ﷺ, nor have I smelt a perfume or any scent sweeter than his ﷺ. I have served the Messenger of Allah for ten years, and in that time, he has never grumbled at me, or told me about something I have done: "why did you do that?" or anything I have not done: "why didn't you do such and such?"

Abdullah Ibn Salam said: "When the Prophet ﷺ arrived at Al-Madinah, everyone rushed to meet him, and when I saw him, I realized his face was not that of a liar."

The Prophet's Pure Morals

Allah ﷻ said: ﴿Nun. By the Pen and by the Record which men write, you are not, by the Grace of your Lord, mad or possessed. Nay, verily for you is a Reward unfailing, and surely you have sublime morals﴾[1], and in the Sahih books, 'Aisha ﷺ said: "The morals of the Prophet ﷺ were Al-Qur'an". Meaning that he ﷺ committed himself to do exactly what the Qur'an ordered him to do, and distanced himself from all that was prohibited; consequently, his willingness to execute the commands of his God was the sublimest of all morals. Allah ﷻ said: ﴿Verily this Qur'an is a guide to that which is most right﴾[1], therefore, his morals were the most honoured, the most noble and the greatest:

- He ﷺ was the most courageous among the people[2] and the bravest in the heat of battles.

- He ﷺ was the most generous, and the highest level of his generosity is displayed in Ramadan[3].

---

[1] Surah Al-Qalam, verse 1-4.
[1] Surah Al-Isra' (also called Bani Israel), verse 9.
[2] Transmitted by Al-Bukhari (3040) and Muslim (2307), on the authority of Anas Ibn Malik ﷺ.
[3] Transmitted by Al-Bukhari (6) and Muslim (2308), on the authority of Ibn 'Abbas ﷺ.

45

- Of all creatures, he ﷺ was the most learned about Allah ﷻ, the most eloquent in speech and the most clement and patient to others.

- He ﷺ was the most decent and the most modest; Qailah Bintu Makhramah said in a Hadith transmitted by Abu Dawud: "And when I saw the Prophet ﷺ sitting in the most humble way (an example to his submission to Allah ﷻ), I trembled with fear"[4].

- And in 'As-Seerah'[5] by Ibn Hisham, the Prophet ﷺ was extremely modest on the day he conquered Makkah; he ﷺ was bowing his head so low that his beard was touching the front of his mount.

- He ﷺ was shier than the virgin in her boudoir[1], but he was the sternest in matters of Allah's sanctity and religion.

- Allah ﷻ praised his companions when He said: ﴿Muhammad is the Messenger of Allah; and those

---

[4] A sound Hadith transmitted by Abu Dawud (4847), on the authority of Qailah Bintu Makhramah.

[5] It has a weak chain. It was transmitted by Ibn Hisham in 'As-Seerah' (12-13/4), on the authority of Ibn Ishaq and of Abdullah Ibn Abu Bakr, and it is Mursal. Also transmitted by Abu Ya'la (3393) and Al-Hakim (47/3), on the authority of Anas Ibn Malik, and its chain is weak.

[1] Transmitted by Al-Bulhari (3562) and Muslim (2320), on the authority of Abi Sa'eed Al-Khudri ﷺ.

who are with him are strong against Unbelievers, but compassionate towards each other⟩[2]

---

[2] Surah Al-Fath, Verse 29.

The Prophet's Journeys

The Prophet ﷺ travelled to Syria twice. His first visit was in the company of his uncle Abu Talib on a commercial trip when he ﷺ was twelve years old. It was during that trip that he ﷺ met the priest who informed him of his mission ﷺ and the Signs of his prophethood, which dazzled everyone's mind. The details of the trip are well laid out in a Hadith transmitted by Attirmidhi[1], on the only authority of Qurad Abu Nuh, with an authentic chain.

The second visit was on a commercial trip that belonged to Khadijah Bintu Khuwailid, accompanied by his servant Maisarah. He went as far as the land of Busrah, sold the goods and returned to Makkah.

The Prophet ﷺ went on a nocturnal journey from Al-Haram Mosque in Makkah to Al-Aqsa Mosque in Palestine, where he gathered with all the Prophets and led them in salat, then on the back of Jibreel عليه السلام he ﷺ flew to the skies, and saw the Prophets, each in his position. He ﷺ exchanged greetings with them, then he ﷺ reached Sidrat Al-Muntaha (the highest level in the seventh heaven) where he ﷺ saw Jibreel (Gabriel) عليه السلام as Allah ﷻ created him; he had six hundred wings. He ﷺ witnessed the great Signs of Allah ﷻ ﴿for truly

---

[1] A sound Hadith transmitted by Attirmidhi (3699), Al-Hakim in his 'Al-Mustadrak' (615/2) and Al-Baihaqi in 'Ad-Dala'il' (24-26/2), its authorities are trustworthy.

did he see, of the Signs of his Lord, the Greatest!}[2]
Allah 🕮 spoke to him and this is the widely known
account of the Specialists in the Prophet's traditions,
and according to a few of them, he 🕮 actually saw his
God 🕮; this is the opinion of Al-Imam Abu Bakr Ibn
Khuzeemah and he was similarly followed by a group
of the latest scholars. Muslim transmitted on the
authority of Ibn 'Abbas that the Prophet 🕮 had seen his
God with his heart twice. Aisha 🕮 denied that the
Ru'ya (seeing Allah) was with the Prophet's naked
eyes; and Muslim transmitted another Hadith on the
authority of Abi Dharr, who asked the Prophet 🕮: "O
Messenger of Allah! Did you see your God? The
Prophet 🕮 said: I have seen a light, how could I see
Him?"

It is this opinion that a group of scholars adopted in old
and recent times, referring to this Hadith and that of
Aisha 🕮; they said: "This is her widely known account
and none of the Prophet's companions opposed her,
except the narration from Ibn 'Abbas that the Prophet
🕮 had seen God with his heart. The author
(Muhammad Ali Al-Halabi) also adopted this account,
and all that was transmitted to confirm the Ru'yah with
the naked eye is not true, neither transmitted directly or
indirectly on the Prophet 🕮. And Allah Knows Best.

The Prophet 🕮 saw Paradise and the Hell Fire, and all
the great Signs. On the same night, he 🕮 received the
injunction of fifty Salat from Allah 🕮; then, the

---

[2] Surah An-Najm, Verse 18.

number was eventually reduced to five after frequent coming and going visits to Musa (Moses) ﷺ and Allah ﷻ.

The Prophet ﷺ finally returned to earth to Al-Haraam mosque in Makkah, and in the morning, he ﷺ informed his people of all the Signs he had been allowed to see.
The Prophet ﷺ said: 'I heard a call saying: I have terminated my injunction, and I have reduced it and shown mercy upon my slaves. O Muhammad! The word does not change with me, it (the number of daily Salats) is five, and it is fifty'[1]. Such words can only be spoken by the Lord of the Worlds; He ﷻ said addressing Musa ﷺ: ﴾Verily, I am Allah: There is no god but I: So worship me only and establish regular Salat for my remembrance﴿[2]. The Salaf (ancient scholars) said: "This is a strong proof that the word of Allah ﷻ is not created, because such language cannot be attributed to a created self." A group of scholars said that whoever declared that the words of Allah ﷻ (Verily, I am Allah: There is no god but I: So worship me only) is created, is an unbeliever; because it would mean that the created subject would have asked Musa (Moses) ﷺ to worship it, and that is untrue.

The Prophet ﷺ transmitted many Holy Hadiths (Qudsi Hadiths), such as ﴾O slaves of Mine! Each of you is hungry apart from who I fed…﴿, it was transmitted by

---

[1] Transmitted by Al-Bukhari (349) and Muslim (163), on the authority of Anas Ibn Malik and Abi Dharr ﵂.
[2] Surah Taha, Verse 14.

Muslim[1]. It has many similarities, and the scholars singled out a special classification about the Holy Hadiths.

A group of scholars specializing in Hadiths and Usul Al-Fiqh (foundations of Islamic Jurisprudence) claimed that Sunnah (the Prophet's Traditions) is sourced from Wahy (Divine Inspiration), pursuing Allah 🕮's words 〈Nor does he say of his own desire, it is no less than inspiration sent down to him 〉[2]. This issue is confirmed in the books of Usul, and it was proficiently investigated by Al-Hafidh Abu Bakr Al-Baihaqi in his book 'Introduction to the Sunan'.

The Prophet 🕮 had seen Jibreel 🕮 in his real picture during his nocturnal journey, and as a matter of fact, he had seen him in the state he was first created earlier as he (Jibreel) was descending from the sky to the earth, at the beginning of the Revelation; Allah 🕮 said: 〈He was taught by one mighty in power, endued with wisdom, for he appeared while he was in the highest part of the horizon, then he approached and came closer, and was at a distance of but two bow-lengths or nearer〉[1]. According to the authentic view of the commentators of Seerah, the appearance in the verses above was that of Jibreel (Gabriel) 🕮; pursuing the Hadith transmitted in the two Sahih books on the

---

[1] Transmitted by Muslim (2577), on the authority of Abi Dharr 🕮.

[2] Surah An-Najm, Verses 3-4.

[1] Surah An-Najm, Verses 5-9.

authority of 'Aisha ﷺ: she asked the Prophet ﷺ about it, and he ﷺ replied: 'That was Jibreel ﷺ'[2]. This Hadith definitely removed any ambiguity in understanding the verse.

The Prophet ﷺ met all the Prophets, during his nocturnal journey, each in his position in the skies, and he ﷺ was shown the guardian of Paradise and the guardian of Hell, while the Angels escorted him ﷺ from one heaven to another, delivering all sorts of advice and messages to him ﷺ.

It was Jibreel ﷺ sent by Allah ﷺ, who brought down the Revelation (the Quran) to the Prophet ﷺ, and in the two Sahih books, it is reported that the Angel of the mountains visited the Prophet ﷺ and offered to punish Quraish by letting the two mountains (Al-Akhshbain) surrounding Makkah fall on them. The Prophet ﷺ pleaded that he should be patient with them[1]. And in a Hadith in Sahih Muslim, it was an angel who was sent by Allah ﷺ to reveal the last two verses in Surah Al-Baqarah[2].

---

[2] Transmitted by Al-Bukhari (3235) and Muslim (177), on the authority of Aisha ﷺ.

[1] Transmitted by Al-Bukhari (3231) and Muslim (1795), on the authority of Aisha ﷺ, the Prophet ﷺ also said: 'I hope that Allah will let them beget children who will worship Allah Alone, and will worship none besides Him."

[2] Transmitted by Muslim (806) and An-Nassa'i (911), on the authority of Ibn 'Abbas ﷺ.

In his book about the Prophet's Invasions, Al-Umawi transmitted a Hadith he received from his father, narrated by Al-Kalbi on the authority of Ibn 'Abbas ﷺ, saying: "While the Prophet ﷺ was gathering the spoils with Jibreel on his right side, another angel came to him and said: "Allah ﷻ Sends salam unto you". The Prophet ﷺ said: 'He is As-Salam, As-Salam is from Him, and As-Salam is to Him.' The Angel then said: "Allah Says to you: the command was the one offered to you by Al-Hubab Ibn Al-Mundhir". The Prophet ﷺ turned to Jibreel ﷺ and said: "Do you recognise this Angel?" Jibreel ﷺ said: "I do not know all that live in the heaven, but he is a trustworthy and by no means a devil." The command was indeed Al-Hubab's excellent idea when the Muslim army arrived at the watering place in Badr; he ﷺ said: "O Messenger of Allah! If your decision to settle here is a command from Allah, then so be it, but if it is a stratagem for war, it would not be the right place". The Prophet ﷺ replied: "It is a stratagem for war", Al-Hubab ﷺ added: "Let us settle at the last water well and bury the remaining wells, then we would have water and they would not". This was previously mentioned in the Battle of Badr.

Listening to the Revelation From The Prophet ﷺ

The Prophet's companions ؓ in Makkah, in Al-Madinah and all the places he ﷺ conquered personally, all listened to the revelations – whether Quran or Sunnah – from the Prophet ﷺ.

The Jinn (Demons) also listened to the Prophet ﷺ when he was reciting the Quran to his companions in 'Ukad, a Makkan place[1]. They came to him one night and asked him various questions. The Prophet ﷺ stood in their company, witnessed by 'Abdullah Ibn Mas'ud ؓ, (the latter was not sitting visibly to them, he was rather waiting for the Prophet ﷺ behind a surrounding wall to keep out of harm's way)[2]. A group of Jinn embraced Islam ؓ on that particular night.

Jibreel (Gabriel) ؑ once visited the Prophet ﷺ in the shape of a Bedouin man, and he ﷺ spoke to him about Al-Eman (faith), Al-Ehsan (the highest status of

---

[1] Transmitted by Al-Bukhari (773) and Muslim (449), on the authority of Ibn 'Abbas ؓ
[2] Transmitted by Ahmed (455, 458/1), its chain of narration include Abu Zaid and Qais ibn Ar-Rabi', whose narrations are weak.

worshiping Allah ﷻ) and the Signs of the Hour (the Day of Judgment)[1]

.

---

[1] Transmitted by Al-Bukhari (50) and Muslim (9), on the authority of Abu Hurairah. It was also transmitted by Muslim (8), Abu Dawud (4695) and Attirmidhi (2610), on the authority of Omar Ibn Al-Khattab ﷺ.

The Number of the Muslims at The Death of The Prophet ﷺ and The Number of Companions Who Transmitted His Traditions

Al-Imam Abu Abdullah Ashafi'i (May Allah Have Mercy upon him) said: "When the Prophet ﷺ died, the Muslims numbered sixty thousand; thirty thousand in Al-Madinah and thirty thousand elsewhere".

Al-Hafidh Abu Zur'ah 'Ubaidullah Ibn Abd Al-Kareem Arraziy (May Allah Have Mercy upon him) said: "When the Prophet ﷺ died, there were more than a hundred thousand people who had seen him or listened to him.

As for Al-Hafidh Abu Abdullah Muhammad Ibn Abdullah Al-Hakim Annisaburi, he claimed that four thousand companions reported on the authority of the Prophet ﷺ.

The author says: "The scholars had assorted the names of the Prophet's companions separately; such is the case of Al-Bukhari at the beginning of his 'History' volume, of Al-Hafidh Abu Nu'aim Al-Asbahani, Sheikh Abu 'Omar Ibn Abd Al-Barr, and others. Abu Hazm, on his part, classified the names of the companions in a chapter he compiled from a book by

Al-Imam Baqiyah Ibn Makhlad Al-Andalusi, and mentioned the accounts of each of them".

The Attributes of The Prophet ﷺ

This section is about the Prophet's exclusive attributes that were not shared by others. Many scholars reported on this subject in the beginning of their volumes of Marriage, like Al-Imam Ashafi'i.

As-Sumairi, on his part, narrated that Abu Ali Ibn Khairan was quoted as saying that he was prohibited from discussing the Prophet's characteristics regarding the rules of marriage, and also of imamah (leading in Salat); for the simple reason that they are exclusive to the Prophet ﷺ. There are no traditions related to them after his death ﷺ and there is no accurate knowledge as to what should be followed in them; therefore, there is no point in wasting time in speculations. As-Sumairi Abu Amru Ibn As-Salah ended his narration by admitting that it was indeed an unusual account. And Allah Knows Best.

The Imam of Al-Haramain in Makkah said, "The Investigators of the Seerah reported that it is fairly useless to mention the scholars' differences in issues related to the Prophet's personal characteristics, for it does not concern a much needed rule, and there is no room for analogy. The distinctive rules have texts to be adhered to; therefore, to tackle the differences of any issue that has no supporting text is a useless attack on the unknown, that only Allah ﷻ Knows".

Sheikh Abu Zakariyah An-Nawawi, however, said that it is permissible and recommendable to look into the Prophet's special attributes. As for the majority of scholars, they did not criticise what was recorded by Ibn Khairan or Imam Al-Haramain; they instead referred to it to add to the knowledge of the readers and learners. They classified the issue in four categories:

- What was obligatory for him ﷺ but not on others.
- What was forbidden to him ﷺ but not to others.
- What was permissible to him ﷺ but not to others.
- What virtues were specifically assigned to him ﷺ but not to others.

They recorded the rules of marriage and other issues in each one of them, and I have decided to arrange them in a more accessible way with success from Allah ﷻ:

- The Prophet's special characteristics are divided to two sections:
- The characteristics that were specifically assigned to him ﷺ and distinguished him from all other Prophets.
- The rules that were specifically assigned to him ﷺ but not to his ummah.

The Characteristics that were Specifically Assigned to Him ﷺ but not to Other Prophets.

In a Hadith in the two Sahih books[1], on the authority of Jaber ibn Abdullah ibn 'Amru ibn Haram Al-Ansari ﷺ, the Prophet ﷺ said:
"I have been given five things which were not given to any one else before me.

1.   Allah made me victorious by awe, by His frightening of my enemies for a distance of one month's journey.
2.   The earth has been made for me (and for my followers) a place for salat and a thing to perform Tayammum with, therefore anyone of my followers can pray wherever the time of a Salat is due.
3.   The booty has been made Halal (lawful) for me yet it was not lawful for anyone else before me.
4.   I have been given the right of intercession (on the Day of Resurrection).
5.   Every Prophet used to be sent to his nation only but I have been sent to all mankind."

Concerning statement 1, it was said that whenever he ﷺ intended to invade a nation, they would be terrorized of him a month before he set out to meet them, and this blessing was given to none but him ﷺ. And what was

---

[1] Transmitted by Al-Bukhari (335) and Muslim (521), on the authority of Jaber Ibn Abdullah Al-Ansari.

reported in Sahih Muslim in the story of the descent of 'Issa ﷺ that "he will descend at the white minaret on the eastern side of Damascus, wearing two garments lightly dyed with saffron and placing his hands on the wings of two Angels. When he lowers his head, there will fall beads of perspiration from his head, and when he raises it up, beads like pearls will scatter from it. Every non-believer who smells the odour of his body will die and his breath will reach as far as he is able to see". If these were his features before he ﷺ was lifted to Allah ﷻ, then they do not match the Prophet's special attributes; in fact, after his descent to the earth, 'Issa (Jesus) ﷺ would be a follower of the Ummah of Muhammad ﷺ, he ﷺ would rule with the same Revelation of the Prophet ﷺ, and Allah knows best.

Statement 2 is explained in a Hadith transmitted by Al-Imam Ahmed in his Musnad[1], where the Prophet ﷺ said: "The nations which were before us did not worship God in their own premises, they rather used to pray in their churches."

As for Tayamum (ritual ablution when there is no water), which was not offered to previous nations, it was legislated to the Prophet ﷺ and his Ummah as a blessing and mercy from Allah ﷻ.

Statement 3 refers to booty, which Allah ﷻ made lawful to the Prophet ﷺ, and there is reference to the

---

[1] Transmitted by Ahmed (7068), on the authority of Abdullah Ibn 'Amru. And Sheikh Shakir, May Allah ﷻ Have him in His Mercy, said the Hadith has an authentic chain.

nations before him 🌸, who whenever they gained any war booty, used to set aside a part of it, and a fire descending from the sky would burn it.

Statement 4 is about intercession, and with it, the Prophet 🌸 referred to the honored position granted by Allah 🌸 solely to Muhammad 🌸; it is a position envied by both the ancestors and the last of the living. Indeed, all mankind long for the Prophet's intercession for them to ask for Allah's Mercy, to spare them any punishment on the Day of Judgment.

The Prophet 🌸 will be, in fact, the first to enter Paradise before the other Prophets; the guard would then tell him: "I was ordered to let no one in before you"[1]. This is specially attributed only to the Prophet 🌸 among all mankind. The Prophet 🌸, then, will enter Paradise and intercede before Allah 🌸, as it is described in the authentic Hadiths. This is called the First Intercession, which is granted to the Prophet 🌸 alone and not to other Messengers, then, it will be followed by several intercessions, whereby he 🌸 will beg Allah 🌸 for His Mercy to spare those from his ummah who committed major sins from the Hell fire. The other Messengers would then indulge to intercede for the sinners in their nations, indeed, the Angels and righteous believers would contribute as well. It was recorded in a Hadith Qudsi on the authority of Abu Hurairah and Abu Sa'eed Al-Khudri: Allah 🌸 Said: "The Angels interceded, and so did the Prophets and

---

[1] Transmitted by Muslim (197), on the authority of Anas Ibn Malik 🌸.

62

the believers, only the Most of the merciful remain[1]."
The Hadiths about intercessions were recorded by
numerous scholars, notably, Al-Imam Abu Bakr ibn
Khuzeemah in the end of his book 'Tawheed', Al-
Imam Abu Bakr ibn Abi 'Asim in his book 'As-
Sunnah', Attabarani and Abu Musa Al-Madeeni Al-
Asbahani.

There is also reference to the Prophet's first
intercession in a Hadith[2] transmitted by Al-Bukhari in
the book of Zakat, in his Sahih on the authority of
Abdullah ibn Omar ﷺ; he said: "The Prophet ﷺ said,
"A man keeps on asking others for something till he
comes on the Day of Resurrection without a scrap of
flesh on his face." The Prophet added, "On the Day of
Resurrection, the sun will come near (to the people) to
such an extent that the sweat will reach up to the
middle of the ears, so, when all the people are in that
state, they will ask Adam for help, and then Moses,
and then Muhammad ﷺ." The sub-narrator added,
"Muhammad will intercede with Allah ﷻ to judge
amongst the people. He will proceed till he holds the
ring of the door (of Paradise) and then Allah will exalt
him to Maqam Mahmud (the privilege of intercession,
etc.). And all the people of the gathering will send their
praises to Allah." This is the great intercession
assigned to the Prophet ﷺ, he will use it on the Day of
Judgment when people go from one Prophet to another
asking for it, until they come to him ﷺ, he will

---

[1] Transmitted by Al-Bukhari (7439) and Muslim (183).
[2] Transmitted by Al-Bukhari (1475).

63

intercede before Allah 🕌 on behalf of everyone at the scene.

The Prophet 🕌 has other intercessions; among them, to save some people among those who would enter Hell fire, and he 🕌 is the first to intercede in Paradise, as it is narrated by Al-Imam Ahmed on the authority of Anas 🕌[1]. He will intercede for the people of Paradise to be granted higher ranks by Allah 🕌. This intercession is agreed upon by Ahl As-Sunnah and Al-Mu'tazilah, and its evidence is a Hadith, in Sahih Al-Bukhari, a narration of Abu Musa and the circumstance was the death of his uncle in Awtas. The Prophet 🕌 said: ' O Allah! Forgive 'Ubaid, Abu Amir and make him on the Day of Resurrection, superior to many of Your human creatures.'[1]   And when Abu Salamah ibn Abd Al-Asad died, the Prophet 🕌 said: 'O Allah! May You raise his rank in Paradise.'[2]

Statement 5, in which the Prophet 🕌 said: 'Every Prophet used to be sent to his nation only but I have been sent to all mankind', refers to the Qur'an. Allah 🕌 said: ⟨We sent not a messenger except to teach in the language of his own people, in order to make things clear to them⟩[3], He 🕌 also said: ⟨And there

---

[1] Transmitted by Muslim (196) and Ahmed (140/3), on the authority of Anas ibn Malik 🕌.
[1] Transmitted by Al-Bukhari (2884) and Muslim (2498), on the authority of Abi Musa 🕌.
[2] Transmitted by Muslim (920), Abu Dawud (3118) Ibn Majjah (1454) o.t.a.o. Abi Musa 🕌.
[3] Surah Ibraheem, verse 4.

never was a people without a warner having lived among them)[4]. Every Prophet in the past was entrusted to deliver the Message only to his people, and was not required to call for Allah ﷻ elsewhere, as for Muhammad ﷺ, Allah ﷻ said: ⟨Say: "O men! I am sent unto you all, as the Messenger of Allah⟩[5], ⟨This Quran has been revealed to me by inspiration, that I may warn you and all whom it reaches⟩[6], ⟨but those of the sects that reject it, the Fire will be their meeting-place⟩[1], ⟨And say to the People of the Book and to those who are unlearned: "Do you submit yourselves?" if they do, they are in right guidance, but if they turn back, your duty is to convey the Message; and in Allah's sight are all His servants.⟩[2] Indeed several verses in the Quran reflect the universality of the Prophet's Message. He ﷺ was ordered by Allah ﷻ to warn all His creatures, the human and the Jinn, the Arabs and the non-Arabs; the Prophet ﷺ duly obeyed the orders of His Lord, and fulfilled his task by completely delivering the Message to its last word.

The Prophet ﷺ was distinguished from other Prophets, because he ﷺ is their leader, their lecturer, their Imam and the last of the Prophets. Allah ﷻ said: ⟨Behold! Allah took the covenant of the Prophets, saying: "I give you a Book and Wisdom: Then comes to you a Messenger, confirming what is with you; you do

---

[4] Surah Fatir, Verse 24.
[5] Surah Al-A'raf, Verse 158.
[6] Surah Al-An'am, Verse 19.
[1] Surah Hud, Verse 17.
[2] Surah Al-'Imran, Verse 20.

believe in him and render him help" Allah said: "Do you agree and take this my covenant as binding on you?" They said: "We agree." He said: "Then bear witness, and I am with you among the witnesses."}[1] Allah said to all the other Prophets that whatever Books and Wisdom He ﷻ gave them, they would have to believe in Muhammad ﷺ and support him if he was to be sent at the time of any of them. This is a special attribute granted to the Prophet Muhammad ﷺ alone.

The miracles of all other Prophets had terminated in their times, but the miracle of the Prophet Muhammad ﷺ is lasting to the Day of the Judgment; it is the Holy Quran, with its wondrous nature that had defied humans and jinn to produce anything similar.

The Prophet ﷺ was taken on a nocturnal journey to Sidrat Al-Muntaha, then returned to his home in one single night. Other Prophets had made the journey before him ﷺ; it is understood in the incident when Al-Buraq resisted the mounting of the Prophet ﷺ on its back, Jibreel (Gabriel) عليه السلام intervened and said to it: "Stand still, by Allah! Of all those who mounted you, none is better than him"[2] and in another hadith, the Prophet ﷺ said: "I tied my mounting creature (Al-Buraq) in the ring where other Prophets tied theirs"[1]. This meant that they also had been taken to the skies;

---

[1] Surah Al-'Imran, Verse 81.
[2] An Authentic Hadith, transmitted by Attirmidhi (3131) Ahmed (164/3) and Abu Ya'la (3184), on the authority of Anas ﷺ.
[1] Transmitted by Muslim (162) Ahmed (148/3) Abu Ya'la (3375), on the authority of Anas ﷺ.

however, we know that none had reached the most honored level of closeness to Allah ﷻ. This is why his status in Paradise is the highest and the nearest to the Holy Throne; he ﷺ said in the Hadith: "Then beg from Allah Al-Wasilah for me, which is a rank in Paradise fitting for only one of Allah's servants, and I hope that I may be that one."[2]

The Prophet ﷺ would be the first whose grave would open for him to be resurrected on the Day of Resurrection. The Prophet ﷺ said in a Hadith narrated by Abu Sa'eed Al-Khudri[3]: "Do not select me above the other Prophets; for the people will fall unconscious on the Day of Resurrection, then suddenly I will see Moses holding one of the pillars of the Throne." Abu Huraira said: The Prophet ﷺ said, "I will be the first person to be resurrected and will see Moses holding the throne."[1]

The Prophet ﷺ is the owner of the greatest Banner on the Day of Resurrection, he ﷺ and his ummah will be resurrected first and elevated alone high above the ground, and Allah ﷻ will authorize them alone to prostrate themselves in the Congregation place. Abu Musa said: the Prophet ﷺ said: "When Day of Resurrection comes, Allah Will deliver to every

---

[2] Transmitted by Muslim (384) Abu Dawud (523) Attirmidhi (3614), on the authority of Abdellah ibn 'Amru Ibn Al-'As ؓ.
[3] Transmitted by Al-Bukhari (2412), on the authority of Abu Sa'eed Al-Khudri ؓ.
[1] Transmitted by Al-Bukhari (2411), on the authority of Abu Hurairah ؓ.

Muslim a Jew or a Christian and Say: That (i.e. a Christian or a Jew) is your rescue from Hell-Fire."[2]

The Prophet ﷺ was sent as the Messenger of Allah ﷻ from the most honored and glorified place on earth, and the majority of scholars claimed that the grave that held his body is the most honored, and the source of this statement is the event of his death ﷺ. When the Companions ؓ disagreed on the place to bury him; whether in Al-Baqee', or in Makkah, or in Bait Al-Maqdis (Jeruzalem), Abu Bakr ؓ intervened in his familiar way to settle the disagreement by saying that Allah ﷻ had made him die in his most loved place.[1]

---

[2] Transmitted by Muslim (2767). (A Christian or a Jew will enter the Hell fire for every Muslim rescued from it).
[1] transmitted by Attirmidhi (1018).

The Characteristics that were Specifically Assigned to Him ﷺ but not to his Ummah

There are some characteristics that were specially attributed to the Prophet ﷺ but not to his Ummah, and the other Prophets might share some of them. They are described as they come in the books of Fiqh[2]:

The Book of Eeman (Faith)

The Prophet ﷺ was infallible in his sayings and in his deeds, Allah ﷻ wanted him to fulfill the Message; therefore, he was not conveying it out of his own desire, it was no less than divine inspiration sent down to him. Many scholars said that the Prophet ﷺ was not to make use of his own independent judgments and interpretations, because he had the divine text. Others said that he might have used his own independent judgments on certain issues, but with the Help of Allah ﷻ, he would not fail.

Abu Al-'Abbas ibn Al-Qass recorded that the Prophet ﷺ alone was commanded to have the knowledge that all mankind as a whole were expected to learn; simply, because he ﷺ is delivering the Message from Allah the All Hearer, the All Knower. Al-Baihaqi quoted the

---

[2] Fiqh means Jurisprudence in Islam.

69

hadith of Ibn 'Omar 😇 that the Prophet 😇 said: "While I was asleep, I was offered a jug of milk; I drank from it until I could see it running through my nails; then, I gave the rest to Omar bin Al-Khattab." They said: "How have you interpreted that, O Messenger of Allah?' He said: "Knowledge"[1].

The Prophet 😇 was entrusted by Allah 😇 to see what other people could not see around him. 'Aisha 😇 quoted the Prophet 😇 saying to her: "This is Jibreel (Gabriel) 😇, he says Salam to you", she said: "May Salam be upon him; O Messenger of Allah! You see what we could not!?[1] And in another Hadith on her authority, she 😇 quoted the Prophet 😇 saying[2]: "By Allah! If you knew what I know, you would have laughed less, and cried a lot." Al-Baihaqi narrated on the authority of Abu Dharr 😇, that "the Prophet 😇 read ❨Has there not been over Man a long period of time, when he was nothing mentioned❩[3] until he finished it, then, he 😇 said: "I verily see what you do not see and I verily hear what you do not hear; the sky has moaned and it has every right to do so; for, in every spot the size of a finger, there is an angel prostrating itself before Allah 😇. By Allah! If you knew what I know, you would have laughed less and cried a lot, and you

---

[1] Transmitted by Al-Bukhari (82) and Muslim (2391), on the authority of Abdullah ibn Omar 😇.
[1] Transmitted by Al-Bukhari (3217) and Muslim (2447), on the authority of Aisha 😇.
[2] Transmitted by Al-Bukhari (1044) and Muslim (901), on the authority of Aisha 😇.
[3] Surah Al-Insan, verse 1.

would not have enjoyed your women on your beds; instead, you would have climbed up the mountains asking Allah for mercy." Abu Dharr said: "By Allah! I wish I were a tree and be bitten of[4]."

The Prophet ﷺ was ordered by Allah ﷻ to aspire to the Hereafter (Al-Akhirah) ahead of the present life (Duniya), he ﷺ was not to feast his eyes on the pleasures of life that other people indulge in blindly; Allah ﷻ said: ﴿Strain not your eyes wistfully at what We have bestowed on certain classes of them﴾[1] and He ﷻ said: ﴿Do not strain your eyes in longing for the things We have given for enjoyment to parties of them, the splendour of the life of this world, through which We test them; but the provision of your Lord is better and more enduring﴾[2].

The Prophet ﷺ was not to learn poetry; Allah ﷻ said: ﴿We have not instructed the prophet in poetry, nor is it meet for him﴾[3]. Abu Dawud narrated on the authority of Abdellah ibn 'Amru ؓ: "I heard the Prophet ﷺ saying: "I would not have focused on what was revealed on me if I drank on an empty stomach or put on an amulet or spoke poetry of my own.'[4] The Prophet ﷺ did not learn writing, and the scholars said it

---

[4] A Sound Hadith, transmitted by Attirmidhi (2312), ibn Majjah (4190), Ahmad (173/5) and Al-Hakim (510/2), on the authority of Abi Dharr ؓ.

[1] Surah Al-Hijr, verse 88.

[2] Surah Taha, verse 131.

[3] Surah Yassin, verse 69

[4] A weak Hadith, transmitted by Abu Dawud (3869) and Ahmad (223, 167/2), on the authority of Abdullah ibn 'Amru.

was forbidden to him to write; Allah ﷻ said: ﴿Those who follow the Messenger, the unlettered Prophet, whom they find mentioned in their own Scriptures –in the Taurat and the Gospel﴾[1], and he ﷺ said: ﴿And you were not able to recite a Book before this, nor were you able to transcribe it with your right hand; in that case, indeed, would the talkers of vanities have doubted﴾[2]. Some of the scholars though, claimed that before his death, the Prophet ﷺ did actually learn to write, but this claim has no sound proof to support it, apart from one narration from Al-Baihaqi of the Hadith of Abu 'Uqail Yahya Ibn Al-Mutawakil, quoting Mujalid and on the authority of the father of Abdullah ibn 'Awn, who said: "The Prophet did not die until he ﷺ learnt to read and write'[3]. Scholar Asha'bi accepted the Hadith as sound, but the chain of narration contains some weak authorities, such as Yahya and Mujalid. Furthermore, a scholar in the Maghreb claimed that the Prophet ﷺ did actually write the Treaty of Al-Hudaibiyah. This claim raised a wave of criticism towards that scholar to deny it, and most of the scholars distanced themselves from such a claim in their khutbas (lectures) on the mimbars. The scholar thought the Prophet did write the Treaty himself and referred to a narration in Sahih Al-Bukhari: "The

---

[1] Surah Al-'Araf, verse 157.
[2] Surah Al-Ankabut, verse 48.
[3] Transmitted by Al-Baihaqi in his Sunan book (42-43/7) and said: this Hadith is *munqati'* and it includes a group of weak and unknown authorities.

Prophet then wrote: This is what has been ruled by Muhammad Ibn Abdellah ﷺ'[1].

However, the theory known to scholars says that what is *absolute* is always overruled by the *restricted* in the context, in terms of the meaning; therefore, it is clear in the other narration of the above Hadith that it was Ali ؓ who actually wrote the Peace Treaty and not the Prophet ﷺ "The Prophet ﷺ ordered Ali ؓ to write: This is what has been ruled by Muhammad ibn Abdellah ﷺ"[2].

To fabricate traditions and ascribe them to the Prophet ﷺ is a greater sin than to lie to someone else; indeed, one Hadith by the Prophet ﷺ was successively narrated by more than eighty companions ؓ, i.e.: "Whoever tell a lie against me intentionally, then, surely, he should expect a seat in Hell-Fire."[1] It was narrated in the two Sahih books by Ali, Anas, Abu Hurairah and Al-Mugheerah ibn Shu'bah. And in another narration in Sahih Al-Bukhari by Az-Zubair ibn Al-'Awwam, Salamah ibn Al-Akwa' and Abdullah ibn 'Amru ؓ, the Prophet ﷺ said: 'Inform people about my Message, at least one verse from the Qur'an, and there is no harm

---

[1] Transmitted by Al-Bukhari (4251) and Muslim (1783), on the authority of Al-Barra' ibn 'Azib ؓ.

[2] Transmitted by Al-Bukhari (2731,2732) on the authority of Al-Miswar ibn Makhramah and Marwan ibn Al-Hakam, and Muslim (1783), on the authority of Al-Barra' ibn 'Azib

[1] Hadith of Ali ؓ was transmitted by Al-Bukhari (106) and Muslim (1). Hadith Anas ؓ: Al-Bukhari (108) and Muslim (2). Hadith Abu Hurairah: Al-Bukhari (110) and Muslim (3). Hadith Al-Mugheerah ibn Shu'bah: Al-Bukhari (1291) and Muslim (4).

in discussing the history of Bani Israel, but whoever tells a lie against me intentionally, then, surely, he should expect a seat in Hell-Fire."[2] This Hadith was also transmitted by Al-Imam Ahmed in his Musnad on the authority of 'Uthman, Omar, Abu Sa'eed, Wathilah ibn Al-Akwa' and Zaid bin Arqam. Attirmidhi transmitted the same Hadith on the authority of ibn Mas'ud[3]; as for ibn Majjah; he quoted narrations from Jaber and Abu Qatadah[1]. Many scholars of the Prophet's traditions, such as Ibraheem Al-Harbi, Yahya ibn Sa'id, Attabarani, Al-Barraz and ibn Mundah among the early scholars, and ibn Al-Juziy and Yusuf ibn Khalil among the scholars that came after them, have compiled books concerning this particular Hadith. All the scholars have agreed by consensus, that whoever lies against the Prophet intentionally – and approves it – is a kafir (Unbeliever). The scholars differed in their judgment on the one who does it intentionally only; sheikh Abu Muhammad Al-Juwini said he is a kafir, but the majority of scholars were against this judgment. However, if the one who commits such an act (to lie against the Prophet ﷺ intentionally) repents afterwards, are his future narrations to be accepted? There are two opinions in this issue:

---

[2] Hadith Az-Zubair ibn Al-'Awwam was transmitted by Al-Bukhari (107). Hadith Salamah ibn Al-Akwa': Al-Bukhari (109). Hadith Abdullah ibn 'Amru: Al-Bukhari (3461).
[3] Transmitted by Attirmidhi (2659).
[1] Ibn Majjah Transmitted Hadith Jabir (33) and Hadith Abu Qatadah (35).

Ahmed ibn Hanbal, Yahya ibn Mu'in and Abu Bakr Al-Humaidi said the repentant's narrations are to be rejected, for the Prophet ﷺ said: "A lie against me is not to be compared to a lie against anybody else; whoever lies against me should surely expect a seat in the Hell-Fire."[1] They said it is well known that whoever lies against other people has sinned, and it is similar if one lies against the Prophet ﷺ. However, if someone repents after lying against other people, his repentance is accepted by consensus, but the narration of one who lies against the Prophet ﷺ is not to be accepted. Indeed, there is a great difference between lying against him ﷺ and lying against other people. However, the majority of scholars said that the narration of the one who lies against the Prophet ﷺ intentionally is acceptable, because the lie against the Prophet ﷺ with intention is *kufr*(Unbelief), and whoever repents of the kufr, his repentance is acceptable and so his narration. And this is the authentic view on the subject.

Among the characteristics assigned to the Prophet ﷺ is that whoever sees him ﷺ in a dream, has actually seen him in reality; the Prophet ﷺ said: 'Satan cannot simulate my image'[2], and the Prophet ﷺ can only be seen in a dream in his real life appearance, as narrated by Annasa'i on the authority of ibn 'Abbas ﷺ. The scholars agreed that a Hadith reported in a dream is not

---

[1] Transmitted by Al-Bukhari (1291) and Muslim (4), on the authority of Al-Mugheerah ibn Shu'bah ﷺ.
[2] Transmitted by Al-Bukhari (110) and Muslim (2266), on the authority of Abu Hurairah ﷺ.

to be approved, because of the uncertainty of the narrator having received it while in his sleep.

Al-Baihaqi reported in his Sunan that Abu Al-'Abbas said explaining the verse ❨If you join gods with Allah, truly fruitless will be your work❩[1] that this verse is aimed at the Prophet 🌼 himself, and the meaning of futility of one's deeds after committing shirk applies to other people only after their death, for Allah 🌼 said: ❨And if any of you turn back from their faith and in unbelief, their work will bear no fruit❩[2], Al-Baihaqi continued: This is the opinion of Abu Al-'Abbas, but other people of knowledge said that the intended subject in the first verse in the Surah Az-Zumur is someone other than the Prophet 🌼, and the theory in Fiqh states that the absolute is dependent on the restricted to clarify any ambiguity.

The Prophet 🌼 was not to deceive in his gestures and behavior – i.e. to make a gesture with a part of the body while intending the opposite meaning in one's speech to dupe and deceive, and this is categorized as lamz (to give someone a wink, which is forbidden). The story of Abdullah ibn Saad ibn Abi Sarh is a strong proof; the Prophet 🌼 had ruled on the day of the conquest of Makkah that Abdullah ibn Abi Sarh among others were to be executed, and when his foster brother 'Uthman ibn Affane 🌼 brought him to the Prophet 🌼 and said: "O Messenger of Allah! Accept his pledge of allegiance", the Prophet 🌼 waited patiently – hoping

---

[1] Surah Az-Zumur, verse 65.
[2] Surah Al-Baqarah, verse 217.

that one of his companions would rise and kill
Abdullah ibn Saad – then accepted 'Uthman's request.
When Abdullah ibn Saad left the scene in the company
of 'Uthman ⁣, the Prophet ⁣ turned to his companions
⁣ and said: "Was there among you no rightly guided
man to rise and kill that man (Abdullah ibn Saad) when
you noticed I abstained from doing it myself?" They
replied: "O Messenger of Allah! You should have
made a gesture to us", but the Prophet ⁣ said: "It is not
characteristic of the Prophet to have the fraud of the
eyes."[1]

The Book of Purification (Taharah)

The Prophet ⁣ was ordered by Allah ⁣ to perform
wudu' (ablution) for each Salat, and when it became
difficult for him, he was ordered to use Siwak before
each Salat. The source of this report is a narration by
Abdullah ibn Handhalah ibn Abi 'Amir that the
Prophet ⁣ was ordered to perform wudu' for each
Salat whether he ⁣ was in total purification or not, but
when it was difficult for him, he was ordered to use
Siwak[1]. The external meaning derived from the above
Hadith is that the use of Siwak was made obligatory on

---

[1] An Authentic Hadith, transmitted by Abu Dawud (2683)
Annsaa'I (4066) and Al-Hakim in his Mustadrak (45/3), on the
authority of Saad ibn Abi Waqqas ⁣.
[1] A sound Hadith, transmitted by Abu Dawud (48) Ahmad (225/5)
and Ad-Daramiy (168-169/1), on the authority of Abdullah ibn
Handhalah ⁣

the Prophet ﷺ, and this is the authentic opinion of the scholars of Hadith; it was reported by Abu Zakariyah An-Nawawiy, while Sheikh Abu 'Amru ibn Salah approved its authenticity. It was also supported by the narration of Al-Imam Ahmad on the authority of ibn 'Abbas that the Prophet ﷺ said: 'I was ordered to use Siwak repeatedly to such an extent I thought the order would come down on me in a Quranic verse or Divine inspiration.'[1] In another narration on the authority of Ummu Salamah, she said: "The Prophet ﷺ said: "Jibreel (Gabriel) was consistently advising me on using Siwak until I feared I would hurt my teeth"[2], transmitted by Al-Baihaqi and regarded as a sound Hadith by Al-Bukhari. Abdullah ibn Wahb reported on the authority of 'Aisha ﷺ that the Prophet ﷺ said: 'I constantly used Siwak until I feared I would lose my teeth.'[3] This was transmitted by Al-Baihaqi, although the chain of narration has a gap between Al-Muttalib and 'Aisha ﷺ; however, all the authorities in the Hadith are trustworthy.

Furthermore, a sound Hadith narrated by Ahmad on the authority of Wathilah ibn Al-Asqa' removes any uncertainty in the issue; he said: "The Prophet ﷺ said: "I was persistently ordered to use Siwak until I thought

---

[1] An authentic Hadith, transmitted by Ahmad (1/237,285,307,315,337,339-340) and Abu Ya'la (2330,2707), on the authority of Ibn 'Abbas ﷺ.
[2] A sound Hadith, Transmitted by Attabarani (23/251) and Al-Baihaqi (7/49), on the authority of Ummu Salamah
[3] A sound Hadith, transmitted by Attabarani (2/99) and Al-Baihaqi (7/49-50).

it would be written on me'[1]. Therefore, some scholars of Hadith claimed that eventually the use of Siwak was not obligatory on him 鑑, but rather *mustahab*.

Among the Prophet's other characteristics is the fact that sleeping did not abrogate his wudu'; it is transmitted in the Sahih books on the authority of ibn 'Abbas 鑑, who said: "The Prophet 鑑 was in deep sleep when the Muadhin called for Salat; he 鑑 got up, went out and performed Salat without renewing wudu'"[2]. This was confirmed by another Hadith on the authority of 'Aisha 鑑, who asked the Prophet 鑑: "O Messenger of Allah! You sleep before you perform witr?" He 鑑 said: "O 'Aisha! My eyes sleep but my heart does not."[3] The scholars differed on whether the Prophet's wudu' was to be cancelled once he 鑑 touched his women. There were two opinions, and the most widely known is that of the cancellation. However, those who assumed it did not relied on a Hadith by 'Aisha 鑑 and transmitted in Sahih Muslim: she missed the Prophet 鑑 from the bed, and when she sought him in the dark, her hand touched the sole of his feet while he was in the state of prostration, and she recalled him praying: "O Allah! I seek refuge in Your pleasure from Your anger, and in Your forgiveness from Your punishment, and I seek refuge in You from

---

[1] A sound Hadith, transmitted by Ahmad (3/490) Attabarani (22/189-190).
[2] Transmitted by Al-Bukhari (138) and Muslim (763), on the authority of Ibn Abbas 鑑.
[3] Transmitted by Al-Bukhari (1147) and Muslim (738), on the authority of Aisha 鑑.

You, I cannot reckon Your praise, You are as You have Lauded Yourself[1]". 'Aisha was also quoted as saying that the Prophet would sometimes kiss her and set out to perform Salat without renewing wudu'[2] and this particular Hadith was used to specify this characteristic only of the Prophet, but the majority of scholars claim that the context of the Hadith does not qualify it to be assigned only to the Prophet.

Question: Did the Prophet have wet dreams?
The answer is in two ways: Annawawi authenticated the opinion that the Prophet never had wet dreams, and this is supported by a Hadith of 'Aisha, she said: "the Prophet at times used to wake in a state of janaba (major ritual impurity) from sexual intercourse, but not from a wet dream, and then he would take a bath and fast that day.'[1] Nevertheless, the clear view in this issue is that if the question of *Ehtilam* means a bodily discharge, then there is no objection to it, but if it means a state of insanity after being beaten by Satan, then it is far from the truth, because the Prophet is infallible and protected by Allah from such acts.

Abu Al-'Abbas ibn Al-Qas reported that it was not prohibited for the Prophet to stay in the mosque even in a state of janaba, and this narration was supported

---

[1] Transmitted by Muslim (486), Abu Dawud (879) Attirmidhi (4393) on the authority of Aisha.
[2] An authentic Hadith, transmitted by by Abu Dawud (179) Attirmidhi (86) and ibn Majjah (502) on the authority of Aisha.
[1] Transmitted by Al-Bukhari (1930) (1931) (1932) and Muslim (1109), on the authority of Aisha and Um Salamah.

by a Hadith of Salim ibn Abi Hafsah quoting Atiyyah and transmitted by Attirmidhi on the authority of Abu Sa'eed 🕮, who said: "The Prophet 🕮 said: "O Ali! It is not permissible for anyone but you or me to be in a state of ceremonial impurity in the mosque."[2] Attirmidhi said: "The hadith is Hasan and Gharib (sound and strange); we know it only in this narration and Al-Bukhari heard it from me."

The author says the narrations of Atiyyah are weak, and Al-Baihaqi said they are not to be considered and maintained. As for Dirar ibn Surad, he was asked by ibn Al-Mundir about the meaning of this tradition, and replied that the meaning was: "It is not permissible for anyone but you and me to walk through it in a state of ceremonial impurity.' However, to walk through a mosque is in fact permissible to everyone without any restriction, except that there is a claim that it is forbidden for anyone but those two to walk through the Prophet's mosque, and that is why the Prophet 🕮 said: '..in this mosque..' referring to his own mosque, and Allah 🕮 knows best. Mahduj Ad-Dhahliy reported on the authority of Jasrah bint Dujajah, quoting Um Salamah saying: "The Prophet 🕮 entered the place of the court in the mosque and said: "It is not allowable for anyone in a state of janaba to be inside the mosque, nor for the monstrous, except the Messenger of Allah 🕮, Ali, Fatimah, Al-Hassan and Al-Hussein. Truly, I have shown you the names to keep you from going

---

[2] A weak Hadith, transmitted by Attirmidhi (3727), and it was selected among the weak Hadiths by Sheikh Al-Albani (6402).

astray."[1] Al-Bukhari said the authority of Mahduj and Jasrah is questionable, and Al-Baihaqi again transmitted this Hadith with the authority of Isma'el ibn Umayah quoting Jasrah, who received it from Um Salamah, but this chain is not authentic. Therefore, the people of Hadith decided that it was not of the traditions of the Prophet ﷺ, and Al-Imam Abu Al-'Abbas ibn Al-Qas thought it was untrue, And Allah Knows Best.

The Book of Salat

Salat Ad-Duha and Salat Al-Witr were considered as obligatory on the Prophet ﷺ but not on his Ummah; this statement was based on a Hadith transmitted by Al-Imam Ahmad in his Musnad and also Al-Baihaqi, on the authority of Abu Janab Al-Kalbi, of 'Ikremah, of ibn 'Abbas ﷺ, that the Prophet ﷺ said: 'Three were obligatory on me: the slaughter (on the Day of Immolation: 10th Dhel-Hijjah), Al-Witr and the two Rakaat of Ad-Duha.'[1] The majority of the scholars of Hadith relied on this Hadith in the matter of the three

---

[1] A weak Hadith, transmitted by Ibn Majjah (645) and Al-Baihaqi (7/65), on the authority of Um Salamah. Sheikh Al-Albani classified the Hadith among the weak traditions of Ibn Majjah (137).

[1] A weak Hadith, transmitted by Ahmad (231/1), Al-Baraz (2433) and Ad-Daraqutni (21/2), on the authority of ibn 'Abbas, however, Abu Janab is weak and a cheat. Sheikh Al-Albani classified this Hadith in his compiler of weak traditions (2561), and said it is fabricated.

commands mentioned, and claimed they were obligatory for the Prophet ﷺ.

Sheikh Taqiy Eddin ibn As-Salah said: "The Scholars of Hadith hesitated to conclude in the matter of Siwak, but they affirmed confidently the obligation of Salat Ad-Duha, Salat Al-Witr and the slaughter in Eid Al-Adha on the Prophet ﷺ, even though their reference is the weak Hadith mentioned above; its weakness comes from its authority Abu Janab Al-Kalbi. Nevertheless, some scholars of Hadith thought he was trustworthy, and Allah Knows Best.

The author says: the majority of scholars of Jarh & Ta'deel agreed about the weakness of that Hadith.

Sheikh Abu Zakariya An-Nawawi reported that some scholars showed hesitations concerning the aspect of the three mentioned obligations as far as the Prophet ﷺ was concerned, and some of them said they were recommendable on him ﷺ. And this view is the predominant one for two reasons:
1.   The Hadith is weak and does not fully support the rule of obligation, furthermore, it was transmitted in another narration on the authority of Mundil ibn Ali Al-'Anazi[1], who is worse than Abu Janab.

---

[1] Weak, Transmitted by ibn Al-Juziy in Al-'Ilal (453/1), on the authority of ibn 'Abbas ﷺ, the chain include Waddah ibn Yahya, of whom ibn Hibban said he was not reliable.

2.   Regarding Al-Witr, it was confirmed in the two Sahih books[2], on the authority of ibn 'Omar that the Prophet ﷺ used to perform it while riding his she-camel, and this is the proof we present the Hanafis that Witr is not obligatory, because if it were obligatory he ﷺ would not have performed it on the back of his she-camel; therefore, his course on this case is that of the plenipotentiary (i.e. acting with the full authority of Allah ﷻ), and Allah ﷻ Knows Best.

As for Salat Ad-Duha, it was reported on the authority of 'Aisha ؤin the two Sahih books[1], that the Prophet ﷺ would not perform it until he came back from his travels. Therefore, if it were obligatory on him, he ﷺ would have observed it regularly.

Salat al-qiyam or Tahajjud[2] is Al-Witr according to authentic traditions; it was narrated by Imam Ahmad on the authority of ibn 'Omar that the Prophet ﷺ said: "Al-Witr is one Rakaa in the night's final hour."[3] This Hadith has a sound chain of authorities. The majority of the scholars of traditions agreed that Tahajjud was

---

[2] Transmitted by Al-Bukhari (999) and Muslim (700), on the authority of Ibn Omar ؤ.

[1] Transmitted by Muslim (717) and Abu Dawud (1292), on the authority of Aisha ؤ.

[2] Tahajjud: Voluntary Salats performed at night between 'Isha and Fajr.

[3] Transmitted by Muslim (752), Abu Dawud (1421), An-Nassa'i (1288) (1289) (1290) and Ahmad (311,361/1), on the authority of Ibn Omar ؤ.

obligatory for the Prophet ﷺ, firmly referring to the verse ﴾And in some parts of the night, also offer Salat with it (Recite Quran in Salat) as an additional Salat for you (O Muhammad ﷺ). It may be that your Lord will raise you to Maqam Mahmud (the highest degree in Paradise)﴿[4]. 'Atiyyah ibn Sa'eed Al-'Awfi transmitted on the authority of ibn 'Abbas, explaining ﴾Additional Salat for you﴿: "It is specially addressed to the Prophet ﷺ, he was ordered to perform Salat Al-Qiyam and it was written on him ﷺ". 'Urwah narrated on the authority of 'Aisha ؓ: "When Allah's Messenger ﷺ occupied himself in Salat, he observed such a long qiyam (posture of standing in Salat) that his feet were swollen. 'Aisha said: O Messenger of Allah! You do this in spite of the fact that your earlier and later sins have been pardoned for you? Thereupon, he ﷺ said: 'Aisha, should I not prove to be a thanksgiving servant (of Allah)?"[1]; this Hadith was also transmitted differently on the authority of Al-Mugheerah ibn Shu'bah.

Al-Baihaqi reported a Hadith[2] by Musa ibn Abderrahman Assana'ni on the authority of 'Aisha, she said: "The Messenger of Allah ﷺ said: "Three were made obligatory for me, and were Sunnah to you: Al-Witr, Siwak and Al-Qiyam". Later, he said Musa ibn

---

[4] Surah Al-Isra',verse 79.

[1] Transmitted by Muslim (2820) and Al-Bukhari (4837), on the authority of 'Urwah ؓ.

[2] A very weak Hadith, transmitted by Al-Baihaqi (39/7), on the authority of Aisha ؓ, its chain is weak, it include Musa ibn Abderahman who is not trustworthy. His narrations are rejected.

Abderahman is very weak, and there is no tracing back to prove it.

Sheikh Abu Hamid reported on the authority of Imam Shafi'i: "Salat Qiyam at night was abrogated for the Prophet ﷺ as it was on the whole Ummah, for it was obligatory on the whole Ummah at the beginning of Islam". Sheikh 'Amru ibn As-Salah said: "This is the true opinion that is supported by many a tradition; such as a Hadith of Saad ibn Hisham on the authority of 'Aisha ﺎ, and it is known to be authentic; it was also similarly reported by Abu Zakariya Annawawi.

The author says: the Hadith mentioned above was transmitted by Muslim and narrated by Saad ibn Hisham, who visited 'Aisha, the Mother of Believers, and said: "O Mother of believers! Inform me about the observance of Salat Al-Qiyam of the Messenger of Allah ﷺ". She said: "Do you not recite ﴾O you wrapped up (i.e. the Prophet ﷺ)﴿?" I said Yes. She said: "Allah ﷻ made the observance of the night Salat at the beginning of this Surah obligatory, so the Messenger of Allah and his Companions around him observed this for one year. Allah ﷻ held back the concluding part of this Surah for twelve months, then he ﷺ revealed the concluding verses, which lightened the burden of this Salat and made it a voluntary (optional) Salat after it was an obligatory one."[1] Ashafi'i referred to the verse ﴾ And in some parts of the night, also offer Salat with it (Recite Quran in

---

[1] Transmitted by Muslim (746) and Abu Dawud (1342), on the authority of Aisha ﺎ.

Salat) as an additional Salat for you⟩[2], and said: "He ﷺ instructed His Messenger that Salat Qiyam was supererogatory and not obligatory, and Allah ﷻ Knows Best".

When the Prophet ﷺ happened to miss the two rakaat after Salat Ad-Duhr, he ﷺ would perform them after Salat Al-'Asr. He used to observe them regularly, as confirmed in the Sahih books[3].

The Prophet's voluntary Salat in sitting position is considered the same as his Salat standing if he ﷺ did not have a 'udr (excuse), as opposed to the rest, for whom it is regarded only as a half Salat. The scholars derived this ruling from a tradition transmitted by Muslim on the authority of Abdullah ibn 'Amru ﵁, who said: "It was narrated to me that the Messenger of Allah ﷺ had said that Salat observed by a person sitting is half of the Salat. So I came to him and found him performing Salat in a sitting position; I placed my hand on his head. He ﷺ said: "O Abdullah ibn 'Omar! What is the matter with you?" I said: "Messenger of Allah, it has been narrated to me that you said: "The Salat observed by a person sitting is half of the Salat,

---

[2] Surah Al-Isra', verse 79.
[3] Transmitted by Al-Bukhari (4370) and Muslim (834), on the authority of Um Salamah. And Muslim transmitted also on the authority of Aisha ﵂, who said: "He ﷺ used to perform them before Asr, but if he was hindered from doing so, or he forgot them, then he would observe them after Asr; it was his habit that whenever he ﷺ performed a Salat, he continued observing it."

87

whereas you are observing Salat sitting". He ﷺ said: "Yes it is so, but I am not like anyone amongst you."[1]

The Prophet ﷺ, at first, did not perform Salat on a person who died leaving behind an unpaid debt; this was transmitted by Al-Bukhari in his Sahih on the authority of Salamah ibn Al-Akwa', but the scholars differed on whether it was forbidden to him ﷺ to do so or just reprehensible, however, this Hadith was abrogated afterwards by another Hadith, whereby the Prophet ﷺ said: "He who died and left behind his wealth, then it is to his inheritors, and he who left behind debt and dependants, then I will take care of them."[1] It was said the Prophet ﷺ used to pay the debt on behalf of the deceased out of obligation, and that he ﷺ did this to honour the dead believers. Furthermore, when the Prophet ﷺ prayed for the dead Muslims, Allah ﷻ enlightened their graves with the blessings of his Messenger ﷺ; this was confirmed in Sahih Muslim [2].

The Prophet ﷺ once passed by two graves, and those two persons (in the graves) were being tortured. He said, "They are being tortured not for a great sin. He then took a green leaf of a date palm, split it into two pieces and fixed one on each grave. The people said,

---

[1] Transmitted by Muslim (735) and Abu Dawud (950), on the authority of Abdullah ibn Omar ﷺ.
[1] Transmitted by Al-Bukhari (2298) and Muslim (1219), on the authority of Abu Huraira ﷺ
[2] Transmitted by Muslim (956), on the authority of Abu Huraira ﷺ.

88

"O Allah's Apostle! Why have you done so?" He replied, "Hoping Allah May lessen their punishment until they (the pieces of the leaf) become dry."[3]

The Prophet ﷺ once had a high fever, and was visited by Abdullah ibn Mas'ud ﷺ, who touched him and said, "You have a very high fever". The Prophet ﷺ said, "Yes, as much fever as two of you may have." Ibn Mas'ud said, "Is it because you have a double reward?" He said, "Yes"[1]. The Prophet ﷺ was invited by Allah ﷻ to choose between having his life extended and then entering Paradise or meeting his Lord in the quickest way; his choice was to leave this worldly life and meet Allah ﷻ[2].

Allah ﷻ had forbidden the earth from eating the bodies of the Prophets, and this statement is illustrated in the Hadith[3] of Shaddad ibn Aws in the Sunan books, and the scholars authenticated it.

---

[3] Transmitted by Al-Bukhari (216) and Muslim (292), on the authority of ibn Abbas ﷺ.
[1] Transmitted by Al-Bukhari (5647) and Muslim (2571), on the authority of Abdullah ibn Mas'ud ﷺ.
[2] Transmitted by Al-Bukhari (4435) and Muslim (2444), on the authority of Aisha ﷺ.
[3] An Authentic Hadith, transmitted by Abu Dawud (1047), Annasa'I (1373) and Ibn Majjah (1085) (1636), on the authority of Ibn Aws. It was reported by Sheikh Al-Albani in the Sahih (2212).

The Book of Zakat

It was forbidden to the Prophet 鏡 to benefit from
sadaqa (almsgiving), whether received as fard
(obligation) or voluntarily; he 鏡 said: "*Sadaqa* was
made unlawful to benefit from for Muhammad and the
family of Muhammad."[1] Muslim reported on the
authority of Abu Huraira 鏡 that the Prophet 鏡 would
eat from a gift but not from *sadaqa*. However, Shafii'
said that it was made legal for the Prophet 鏡 to benefit
from voluntary *sadaqa*; this statement was narrated by
Seikh Abu Hamid. After the death of the Prophet 鏡,
some Arab Bedouins concluded that Zakat was to be
paid only to the Prophet, and refused to pay it to Abu
Bakr As-Siddiq until he 鏡 fought them and made them
comply with the truth. The scholars have issued books
to provide their answers on the subject.

The Book of Siyam (Fasting)

The Prophet 鏡 was permitted to perform Al-Wisal
(fasting continuously for more than one day without
taking any meals), and forbade it on his Ummah. A
man from the Muslims said, "But you do Al-Wisal, O
Messenger of Allah!" the Prophet said, "Who among
you is similar to me? I sleep and my Lord makes me

---

[1] Transmitted by Muslim (1072), on the authority of Al-Muttalib
ibn Rabee'ah ibn Al-Harith 鏡.

eat and drink."1   The companions ﷺ were eagerly in favour of fasting continuously, but he ﷺ convinced them that Al-Wisal was specifically authorized to him by Allah ﷻ, Who provided food and drink for him. The scholars differed as to whether the feeding was material or spiritual. There are two opinions, and the more authentic one was that the feeding was spiritual; otherwise Al-Wisal would not have taken place.

The Prophet ﷺ was permitted to kiss his wives while he was fasting[2] . It was a special attribute to him ﷺ; and the question is: is it forbidden to the rest of the Muslims? Or undesirable? Or lawful? Does it nullify one's siyam if one does it, as was claimed by ibn Quteebah? Or is merely Mustahab (recommendable, desirable)? Does the law distinguish between old and young people? The scholars have all had their say on these particular points.

An issue concerning the voluntary siyam of the Prophet ﷺ: some scholars said that whenever he started one, he would observe it until its completion; however, this is a weak Hadith cancelled by an authentic one in Sahih Muslim on the authority of 'Aisha ﷺ: Once the Prophet ﷺ entered the house, and she said: "O Messenger of Allah! Here is some soup", he said:

---

[1] Transmitted by Al-Bukhari (1961) and Muslim (1104), on the authority of Anas ﷺ

[2] Transmitted by Al-bukhari (1928) and Muslim (1106), on the authority of 'Aisha ﷺ.

"Bring it to me, for I woke up fasting this morning'1 and he 鬱 ate from it.

The Book of Al-Hajj

Some scholars said: whenever the Prophet 鬱 witnessed something he liked, he would say: "O Allah! The real life is that of the Hereafter" And this is based on the Hadith transmitted by Al-Bukhari and narrated by Sahl ibn Saad, who said: "We were in the company of the Prophet 鬱 on the day of the battle of Al-Khandaq; the Prophet 鬱 was digging the trench and we were removing the ground; then he caught sight of our efforts and said: "O Allah! The real life is that of the Hereafter, so please forgive the Ansars and the Emigrants." [1]

Makkah was made lawful to the Prophet 鬱 for one day, he entered it without ihram, and around twenty Makkan people died in the conquest. Was its conquest attained by force? Or was it through a peace deal? It was indeed a victory granted from Allah 鬱 to his Messenger; he 鬱 said on the second day of the conquest after praising Allah 鬱: "Makkah has been

---

[1] Transmitted by Muslim (1154) and Abu Dawud (2455), on the authority of Aisha, the mother of believers.
[1] Transmitted by Al-Bukhari (4098) and Muslim (1804), on the authority of Sahl ibn Saad 鬱. It was also transmitted by Al-Bukhari (3795) and Muslim (1805), on the authority of Anas ibn Malik 鬱.

made a sanctuary by Allah and not by the people, so it is not lawful for a person who believes in Allah and the Last Day to shed blood in it, or to cut down its trees, and if someone asks permission to fight in Makkah because Allah's Apostle was allowed to fight in it, say to him: "Allah permitted His Apostle and did not allow you".[2]

The Book of Food

Some scholars said that it was forbidden for the Prophet ﷺ to eat onions, garlic and leek, and they support their statement with a Hadith by Jaber, that when the Prophet ﷺ was offered a pot of vegetables and herbs, he ﷺ ordered that it should be brought near to some of his Companions who were with him. When he ﷺ saw they disliked eating it as well, he said, "Eat. (I don't eat) for I converse with those whom you don't converse with (i.e. the angels)." This Hadith had led some scholars to assume that onion and garlic were two vegetables the Prophet ﷺ was not allowed to eat, and they referred to a narration of Ali ﷺ, transmitted by Attirmidi[1]. However, the authentic view is that they are not forbidden for the Prophet ﷺ, it was instead

---

[2] Transmitted by Al-Bukhari (104) and Muslim (1354), on the authority of Abu Sharih Al-Khuzai' ﷺ.

[1] An authentic Hadith, transmited by Attirmidi (1808) (1809) and Abu Dawud (3828), on the authority of Ali ﷺ, he said: "it is forbidden to eat garlic unless it is cooked", and in another narration: "Garlic should only be eaten cooked".

undesirable and unpleasant; and the proof lies in the Hadith transmitted by Muslim on the authority of Abu Ayyub: he once prepared a meal with garlic, but the Prophet ﷺ rejected it and did not eat from it. Abu Ayyub asked: "Is it Haram?" the Prophet ﷺ said: "No, but I dislike it", Abu Ayyub then said: "I dislike what you dislike". Sheikh Abu Amru said that this Hadith nullifies any prohibition therein. And Allah Knows Best.

The Prophet ﷺ said, concerning eating lizard: "I do not eat it nor make it unlawful." Ibn Abbas reported: "I and Khalid ibn Walid went to the apartment of Maymunah along with Allah's Messenger ﷺ, and there was presented to him a roasted lizard. Allah's Messenger ﷺ stretched his hand towards it, whereupon some of the women who had been in the house of Maymunah said: Inform Allah's Messenger ﷺ what he intends to eat. The Prophet ﷺ lifted his hand. I said: "Messenger of Allah, is it forbidden?" He said: "No. It is not found in the land of my people, and I feel that I have no liking for it". Khalid said: "I then chewed and ate it, while Allah's Messenger ﷺ was looking (at me)"."[1] Therefore, it is undesirable for anyone to eat something they dislike, for the Prophet ﷺ said: "What is loathsome leads to harm and waste", and even doctors advise against eating what is undesired.

Al-Bukhari reported on the authority of Abu Juhaifa that the Prophet ﷺ said: "I do not take my meals while

---

[1] Transmitted by Al-Bukhari(5391) and Muslim (1946), on the authority of Khalid Ibn Al-Walid ﷺ.

leaning."[1] Some scholars said it was prohibited on him, but Annawawi said: the authentic opinion is that it was undesirable for him, not unlawful. The author says therefore, this statement does not apply specifically to the Prophet ﷺ; indeed, it is undesirable for everyone to take meals in a leaning position, considering the harm it might generate. The Prophet ﷺ was prohibited from drinking while standing, because it denotes arrogance and oppression, and Allah Knows Best.

Abu Al-Abbas ibn Al-Qas said that the Prophet ﷺ was prohibited from attending and eating a meal without being invited as a guest; he ﷺ said in a Hadith transmitted by Abu Dawud on the authority of ibn Omar: "He who was invited to a meal and did not turn up, has indeed disobeyed Allah and his Messenger. And he who attends a meal without any invitation, has entered as a thief and walked out as an invader."[1]

The scholars said that it was obligatory that whoever was asked for a particular meal he did not have should spare no effort to provide it for the Prophet ﷺ, to uphold the Prophet's life and noble self, for Allah ﷺ said: ﴾The Prophet is closer to the believers than their

---

[1] Transmitted by Al-Bukhari (5398), Abu Dawud (3769) and Attirmidi (1830), on the authority of Abu Juhaifa ﷺ.
[1] Transmitted bu Abu Dawud (3741) and Al-Baihaqi (7/68, 265), on the authority of Ibn Omar, and it is a weak chain. Sheikh Al-Albani mentioned it among the weak Hadiths of Abu Dawud (798). However, the first part of the Hadith is authentic, it was transmitted by Al-Bukhari and Muslim.

own selves⟩². The author says the meaning of this ayah resembles the Hadith that is transmitted in the two Sahih books: "None of you is to be considered a believer until I become more beloved to him than his son, his father and all mankind."³

The Issue of Gifts

The Prophet ﷺ used to accept presents from people and reward them generously, as it was confirmed in the Sahih books¹ on the authority of 'Aisha ◈. His wish was always to reconcile the heart of whoever gave him a gift and pray for them; as for other emirs and leaders, the presents given to them are regarded as treachery in the spoils and thieving from the booty before its division, because it is considered as a suspicious bribery², and Allah Knows Best.

Zakariya ibn 'Uday reported that ibn Abbas said explaining the verse ⟨and that which you give in gift (to others) in order that it may increase (your wealth by expecting to get a better one in return from other

---

² Surah Al-Ahzab, verse 6.
³ Transmitted by Al-Bukhari (15) and Muslim (44), on the authority of Anas Ibn Malik ◈.
¹ Transmitted by Al-Bukhari (2585), Abu Dawud (3532) and Attirmidi (1953), on the authority of Aisha ◈.
² An Authentic Hadith, transmitted by Ahmad (424/5) and Al-Baihaqi (138/10), on the authority of Abu Hamid Assa'idi. Sheikh Al-Albani Said in 'Irwa' Al-Ghalil' (2622): it is authentic.

96

people's property), has no increase with Allah》[3]: "It is lawful usury – one gives a present and expects a better one in return – however, there is no reward in it from Allah ﷻ, but no misdeed either". The Prophet ﷺ was prohibited from engaging in this type of gift; Allah ﷻ said: ﴾and give not a thing in order to have more﴿[1]; this Hadith was transmitted by Al-Baihaqi on the authority of Al-Hakim.

Among the religious obligations revealed to the Prophet ﷺ was the fact he ﷺ was not to make a will, and whatever he ﷺ left behind was *sadaqa*. It was transmitted in the two Sahih books on the authority of Abu Bakr ؓ that Fatima ؓ asked him about the inheritance from her father ﷺ. Abu Bakr ؓ said: "I heard the Prophet ﷺ saying: 'We Prophets are not to make a will, and whatever we leave is to be given in charity', but the family of Muhammad can take their sustenance from this property. And I, By Allah, would not change anything in the *sadaqa* of the Prophet ﷺ, and will keep them as they used to be observed in his life-time."[2] And in another Hadith on the authority of Abu Huraira, the Prophet ﷺ said: "My heirs should not take even a single Dinar (i.e. anything from my property), and whatever I leave, excluding the expenditure of my wives and my laborers, will be

---

[3] Surah Ar-Rum, verse 39.
[1] Surah Al-Mudathir, verse 6.
[2] Transmitted by Al-Bukhari (3093) and Muslim (1759), on the authority of Abu Bakr As-Siddiq ؓ.

sadaqa (i.e. be used for charity)"[1]. Ahlu Al-Hal wal 'Aqd (the influential prominent scholars) have all agreed that the Hadiths above are the answers to the issue of the inheritance from the Prophet's property; therefore, it is needless to refer here to the fictitious and fabricated stories raised by the Shiites and Rafidites, whose ignorance had spread far and wide.

The Book of Nikah (Marriage)

This book include the general rules of the appropriations and allowances of the Prophet ﷺ concerning nikah; they are mentioned in well arranged sections, the way they were highlighted by the scholars:

---

[1] Transmitted by Al-Bukhari (3096) and Muslim (1760), on the authority of Abu Huraira ﷺ.

Section 1: What Was Obligatory For Him ﷺ but not on Others

Allah ﷻ ordered him to grant his wives the option or choice; He ﷻ said: ❴O Prophet, tell your wives: "If you desire the life of the dunya and its finery, come and I will give you all you need and release with kindness. But if you desire Allah and his Messenger and the abode of the Akhira, Allah has prepared an immense reward for those among you who are doers of good."❵[1], it was also issued in the two Sahih books on the authority of 'Aisha ؓ[2]. The scholars differed on whether the granting of choice or option was obligatory on him or recommendable. Annawawi and others suggested strongly that it was an obligation on him ﷺ. The scholars also differed on whether the Prophet's wives had to make an immediate reply or at their leisure? Ibn Assabagh said: there is no dispute that the Prophet ﷺ had enabled Aisha to choose at her leisure when he ﷺ said to her: "you are allowed to consult your parents".

When the wives made their choices to be his wives, was the Prophet ﷺ prohibited from divorcing them? The scholars suggested firmly that it was not forbidden; however, Allah ﷻ, at first, denied him other women as a good reward to the Prophet's wives (for they chose Allah, his Prophet and the Hereafter), then

---

[1] Surah Al-Ahzab, verse 28.
[2] Transmitted by Al-Bukhari (4785) and Muslim (1475), on the authority of Aisha ؓ.

99

He ﷺ made it lawful for him ﷺ. 'Aisha ؓ said: "Before his death, other women were made lawful for him to marry' transmitted by Ashafi'.[1]

Section 2: What Was Prohibited For Him to Marry but not for Others:

The scholars said that it was prohibited for the Prophet ﷺ to hold on to any wife who chose to separate from him. Another person, on the other hand, would grant his wife the choice, and if she chose to separate from him, then, he should not agree to her choice, and Allah ﷻ Knows Best. Other scholars said the Prophet ﷺ separated from his wife out of his kindness and generosity.

Was it lawful for the Prophet ﷺ to marry a woman from the people of the Book? Annawawi suggested strongly that it was prohibited for him ﷺ, and that was the opinion of ibn Sareej, Al-Istakhri and Abu Hamid Al-Marwarudhi. Sheikh Abu Nasr ibn Assabagh selected as evidence to that opinion the Prophet's Hadith: "My wives in the dunya (this world) are indeed my wives in Al-Akhira (Hereafter)."[2] Then he related

---

[1] Sahih, transmitted by Attirmidi (3212)Annasa'I (3204),Ahmad (6/41), on the authority of Aisha ؓ.
[2] The author said that he did not come across this Hadith in this wording, however, Al-Bukhari transmitted, on the authority of Ammar ibn Yasir ؓ about Aisha ؓ: By Allah! She is truly the wife of your Prophet ﷺ in dunya and Akhira.. Al-Baihaqi reported in his sunan (69-70/7) on the authority of Hudaifa ؓ that he said to his wife: if you want to be my wife in Al-Jannah, do not marry

the other opinion, which is that it was lawful to marry women from the people of the Book, and said that this did not require any evidence because when they (women) married him 🌸; they embraced Islam.

The author believes: the Hadith mentioned above is not traceable to the Prophet 🌸; it was only the words of the Companions, and Abu Ishaq Al-Mirwazi said it is not prohibited.

It was lawful on the Prophet 🌸 to take a woman from the people of the Book as a concubine, but he 🌸 was forbidden from marrying a Muslim female slave.

Section 3: What Was Lawful for Him to Marry but not for Others

When the Prophet 🌸 died, he 🌸 had nine wives; the scholars agreed about the lawfulness of him 🌸 marrying nine women, but they differed as to whether he 🌸 was allowed more wives, and the more authentic view is that it was lawful for him 🌸. Al-Bukhari transmitted on the authority of Anas 🌸, who said: "Tthe Prophet 🌸 used to visit his wives in an hour of day or night, and there were eleven of them(wives), Qatada asked Anas: "Could he endure it all? He said:

---

after me, for the woman in Al-Jannah is to her last man in dunya; therefore Allah 🌸 forbade the Prophet's wives from marrying after him 🌸, because they are his wives in Al-Jannah.

"we used to narrate about him ﷺ having the energy of thirty men", (or forty in another narration)[1].

Al-Bukhari transmitted the same Hadith in a narration of Sa'eed on the authority of Anas, he said[2]: "Tthe Prophet ﷺ had nine wives then." (Anas said he ﷺ married fifteen women in total, he consummated the marriage with thirteen, he once was married to eleven, and died when he ﷺ was married to nine of them)

The scholars said that it was permissible for the Prophet ﷺ to contract the marriage as a deed of gift, for Allah ﷻ said: ❴and a believing woman if she offers herself to the Prophet, and the Prophet wishes to marry her; a privilege for you only, not for the rest of the believers❵[3], and if the marriage was contracted as a deed of gift, then, unlike other marriages, there was no dowry for the contract nor for the consummation. The Prophet ﷺ was authorized to marry women without their guardians or witnesses, following the Hadith of Zainab bint Jahsh, who used to boast before the Prophet's other wives, saying: "You were married by your families, and my marriage to the Prophet ﷺ was contracted by Allah ﷻ from above seven heavens."[1]

---

[1] Transmitted by Al-Bukhari (268), on the authority of Anas ibn Malik ؆.
[2] Transmitted by Al-Bukhari (284), on the authority of Anas ibn Malik ؆.
[3] Surah Al-Ahzab, verse 50.
[1] Transmitted by Al-Bukhari (7420), on the authority of Anas ibn Malik ؆.

Was it lawful for the Prophet ﷺ to marry in a state of ihram (state of ritual consecration)? There are two standpoints:

First: he ﷺ was not allowed to marry in a state of ihram, and this opinion was derived from the generality of the Hadith, transmitted by Muslim on the authority of 'Uthman ⌐, who said: "The Prophet ﷺ said: "He who is in state of ihram is not to marry, nor get married, nor get engaged"."[2]

Second: some scholars authenticated the lawfulness, and this view was based on a Hadith by ibn Abbas ⌐, who said that the Prophet ﷺ married Maimunah in a state of ihram[1]. But this Hadith was opposed by another Hadith reported by Muslim on the authority of Maimunah herself: she said that the Prophet ﷺ married her and they were not in a state of ihram[2]; the owner of the story knows it more than others, and Allah ﷻ knows best.

Was it obligatory for the Prophet ﷺ to divide his time between his wives and his bondmaids? It is clear from the Prophet's traditions that it was obligatory; indeed, he ﷺ used to go about visiting his wives even in a state of illness, until he ﷺ requested their permission to stay

---

[2] Transmitted by Muslim (1409), Abu Dawud (1841) and Attirmidi (840), on the authority of Uthman ibn Abbas ⌐.
[1] Transmitted by Al-Bukhari (5114) and Muslim (1410), on the authority of ibn Abbas ⌐.
[2] Transmitted by Muslim (1411), Abu Dawud (1843) and Attirmmidi (845), on the authority of the mother of believers ⌐.

at the house of 'Aisha 🕮 to be nursed, and they accepted. However, Abu Sa'eed Al-Istakhri claimed that it was necessary for the Prophet 🕮 to share his time evenly with his wives, for Allah 🕮 said: ❨You may refrain from any of them you will, and keep close to you any of them you will❩[3], therefore, it is among his special attributes.

He 🕮 set Safiya free and made it her dowry, as it was confirmed in the two sahih books[4] on the authority of 'Aisha 🕮. It was said that he 🕮 set her free on condition that she married him; therefore, it was obligatory for her to meet the condition; this was the opinion of Al-Ghazali, who said that it was one of the attributes of the Prophet 🕮 but not of others.

Section 4: The Virtues Privileged to The Prophet 🕮 and not to Others.

The Prophet's wives are the mothers of the believers, Allah 🕮 said: ❨the Prophet has closer ties to the believers than their own selves, and his wives are their mothers❩, and the meaning of this motherhood: Respect, obedience, forbidding all sorts of disobedience, and displaying all kind of exaltation and glorification; it was lawful to be alone with them, which is not the case with other Muslim women on whom the sanctity applies (i.e. they should not be

---

[3] Surah Al-Ahzab, verse 51.
[4] Transmitted by Al-Bukhari (5086) and Muslim (1365)

alone with men other than their husbands, sons and brothers).

Are the Prophet's wives the mothers of female believers? 'Aisha ∗ said they are not.

Was the Prophet ∗ called the father of the believers? Al-Baghawi reported on the authority of some scholars that it was permissible. The author says: that is the statement of Mu'awiya; as for Ubai and ibn Abbas ∗, they read ❬ the Prophet has closer ties to the believers than their own selves – and he is their father – and his wives are their mothers❭[1]. However, Al-Waqidi reported that some scholars suggested that he ∗ is not to be called the father of believers, quoting the verse: ❬Muhammad is not the father of any of your men❭[2], but in this verse, the meaning of fatherhood is in terms of the lineage only; for in another Hadith transmitted by Abu Dawud, the Prophet ∗ said: "I am to you rather like a father❭[3]

The Prophet's wives are the best women of the Ummah for their double reward in Al-Jannah, and the best of them all are Khadeejah and 'Aisha ∗. Abu Sa'eed Al-Mutawali said: "The scholars differed on who is the worthier of the two? Ibn Hazm said that the

---

[1] Transmitted by Al-Baihaqi in his Great Sunan (69/7), on the authority of ibn Abbas.
[2] Surah Al-Ahzab, verse 40.
[3] Hadith hasan (good). Transmitted by Abu Dawud (8), Annasa'I (40) and ibn Majjah (313), on the authority of Abu Huraira ∗. Sheikh Al-Albani said in his Sahih Al-Jami' (2346): good.

Prophet's wives are better than all the companions, even better than Abu Bakr Assidiq 🙏, and this statement is very odd and weak, and it has never been quoted by a scholar before him.

It was forbidden to marry the Prophet's wives that he had left behind, because they are his wives in Al-Jannah. And if a woman does not get married after the death of her husband, she will be his wife in Akhira (Hereafter); it was narrated that when Abu Addarda' was in his demise, his wife said to him: "O Abu Addarda'; you asked my family to marry me and they agreed, and I ask you today to remain my husband", he said: "Then do not get married after me. After the death of Abu Addarda', she was approached by Mu'awiya – and he was the Amir – and she refused. [1]

Al-Baihaqi reported on the authority of Hudaifa 🙏, who said to his wife: "Your secret is to be my wife in Al-Jannah (Paradise), so do not marry anyone after me, because the woman in Al-Jannah is to her last man in Dunya". Therefore, it was forbidden for the Prophet's wives 🙏 to be married after him, because they are his wives in Al-Jannah. [2]

And whoever slanders 'Aisha 🙏, the mother of believers, is to be executed, as agreed unanimously by the scholars; this statement was narrated by Assuhaili

---

[1] Sheikh Al-Albani transmitted this hadith among the Sahih traditions (1281).
[2] Transmitted by Al-Baihaqi (69-70/7).

106

and others. Indeed, Allah ﷻ sent downs verses[1] in the Qur'an to prove her innocence of any misdeed.

The death sentence is also on whoever speaks evil of the Prophet ﷺ, whether man or woman; there are indeed many traditions related to this subject, among them a Hadith by ibn Abbas about the blind man who killed his wife, when she backbit the Prophet ﷺ. This incident was reported to the Prophet ﷺ who said: O do be witness that her blood was shed.[2] Shu'bah said on the authority of Abi Barzah: "A man insulted Abu Bakr, and I said: "Should I kill him?" Abu Bakr replied: "It is not for anyone after the Prophet ﷺ" (i.e. that severe judgment applies on whoever insults the Prophet ﷺ but not on insulting other people).[3] Ibn Udai reported a Hadith on the authority of Abu Huraira ﷺ, who said: "None should be killed for insulting anyone, except for insulting the Prophet ﷺ. Sheikh Imam Abu Al-Abbas ibn Taymiyah had issued his highly praised book "As-Saarim Al-Maslul 'ala mann sabba Ar-Rasul ﷺ" to cover this subject.

---

[1] The verses (11-20) in Surah An-Nur, whereby Allah ﷻ praised Aisha ﷺ for her innocence, and promised a terrible punishment to those who spread the lies and accusations about Aisha in Al-Madina.

[2] Hadith Sahih. Transmitted by Abu Dawud (4361), Annasa'I (4081) Al-Hakim (354/4) and others, on the authority of ibn Abbas ﷺ. Sheikh Al-Albani mentioned selected in Sahih Abu Dawud (3665).

[3] A sound hadith, transmitted by Annasa'I (4082) Attayalisi (4) Ahmad (60/7) and Al-Baihaqi (60/7), on the authority of Abu Barzah Al-Aslami. It was reported by Sheikh Al-Albani in Sahih Annasa'I (3795) and Sahih Abu Dawud (3666).

107

The Prophet's Attributes in Jihad

It was characteristic on the Prophet ﷺ that whenever he put on his body armour for the battle, he was not allowed to take it off until the battle was finished. It was on the day of the Battle of Uhud, when his Companions ؓ decided to set out and meet their enemy in Uhud, he ﷺ went inside his house, wore his body armour and when he ﷺ went out, they said: "O Messenger of Allah! If you want you may go back and stay". He ﷺ said: "Once a Prophet puts on his body armour for a war, he is not allowed to return until he has fought."[1] This Hadith was reported by the scholars who wrote about the battles of the Prophet ﷺ, and the majority of them said it was unlawful for him to take off the body armour until he had fought the enemy.

Among the Prophet's characteristics was the obligation to consult his Companions in the war affairs. Allah ﷻ said: ﴾and consult with them about the matter﴿[1] Ashafi' said Sufyan ibn 'Uyainah reported on the authority of Az-Zuhari, he said: Abu Huraira said: "I have never seen anyone consulting his companions intensively than the Prophet ﷺ"[2]. Ashafi' said: Al-

---

[1] A sound Hadith, transmitted by Ahmad (351/3), on the authority of Jabir, also transmitted by Al-Baihaqi (41/7), on the authority of Ibn Abbas.
[1] Surah Al-Imran, verse 159.
[2] Transmitted by Ashafi' and reported by Al-Baihaqi in his Sunan (45/7).

Hasan said: The Messenger of Allah could have acted without consulting his Companions, but he 🌸 wanted the leaders after him to follow his example[3].

The scholars said that it was obligatory for the Prophet 🌸 to stand up to his enemies and endure any suffering, even if his enemy were more than double his own. This view was probably taken from the Hadith of Al-Hudaibiya, where the Prophet 🌸 said to 'Urwah: "But if they (the Quraish) do not accept the truce, by Allah in Whose Hands my life is, I will fight with them defending my cause till I get killed"[1].

The Prophet 🌸 was authorized to deceive his enemies in wars; he 🌸 said: "War is deceit." Indeed, on the day of Al-Ahzab (the Confederates) invasion, he 🌸 ordered Nu'aim to create enmity between Quraish and Quraidah, and their alliance was broken by the Will of Allah, and All Praise is to Allah 🌸.

The Prophet 🌸 had the privilege to choose first from the spoils; he 🌸 would take whatever he wanted: a servant or a bondmaid, or weapon, or anything else before the division of the booty. He 🌸 was entitled to the fifth of the fifth of the booty (taken after a war), and the fourth of the fifth of al-fai' (spoils taken without any fighting).

---

[3] Transmittted by Abu Hatim with a good chain, on the authority of al-Hasan Al-Basri,
[1] Transmitted by Al-Bukhari (2731,2732), on the authority of Al-Miswar ibn Makhrama and Marwan ibn Al-Hakam.

The Prophet's position in judicial rulings:
The scholars said that he ﷺ had the authority to make a ruling based on his knowledge[2] for there was no room for accusations on his part; and the evidence of this point is the Hadith of Hind bint 'Utbah who complained about her husband Abu Sufyan being a miser, and the Prophet ﷺ said to her: "You may take from his money what is sufficient for you and your sons."[1] The scholars added that the Prophet ﷺ was entitled to judge for himself and his children, and to stand witness for himself and his children. His testimony was accepted, as it was the case in Hadith Khuzaima ibn Thabit ﷺ[2].

It is lawful to be named after him ﷺ (Muhammad), as for the use of his surname (Abu Al-Qasim), the scholars had three opinions:

The absolute prohibition to be surnamed (nicknamed) Abu Al-Qasim after the Prophet ﷺ, and this is observed

---

[2] The ruling based on the Prophet's knowledge concerns only simple day to day issues but not 'Hudud'(legal punishments) because they are Divine Ordinances issued by Allah ﷺ. For example, the Prophet ﷺ knew the names of the hypocrites in Al-Madina, but did not punish them because there should be some clear physical evidence of their hypocrisy before the public; therefore, he ﷺ could not make any ruling based on his knowledge.

[1] Transmitted by Al-Bukhari (2211) and Muslim (1714), on the authority of Aisha ﷺ.

[2] A sound Hadith, transmitted by Abu Dawud (3607), Annasa'I (4661) and Al-Hakim (17-18/2). It is also mentioned by Sheikh Al-Albani in Sahih Abu Dawud (3073).

in the Shafi' school; it was reported by Al-Baihaqi and Al-Baghawi and based on a Hadith on the authority of Abu Huraira ⚜, he said: the Prophet ﷺ said: "Name yourselves with my name, but do not name yourselves with my kunya (nickname: Abu Al-Qasim)."[1]

The absolute permission to use his nickname, and this is better practised in the Maliki School, and the view of Annawawi, may Allah's Mercy be upon him. They said the nickname had had its meaning in the life Prophet ﷺ and that it came to an end when he ﷺ died.

It is lawful to use the Prophet's nickname on whoever's name is not Muhammad (and not on those named Muhammad); for one should not combine both the Prophet's name and his surname, and this was the view of Abu Al-Qasim Abd El-Karim Ar-Rafi'.

The scholars said that whoever belittled and despised the Prophet ﷺ in his presence was adjudged a disbeliever, and whoever made little of his true Sunnah after his death – with the condition that he/she knows it is the true Sunnah of the Prophet ﷺ – is adjudged a disbeliever.

Among the Prophet's attributes, the scholars reported that his lineage include the sons of his daughter; in reference to a Hadith transmitted by Al-Bukhari on the authority of Abu Bikrah ⚜, who said: "I saw the Messenger of Allah on the pulpit and Al-Hasan ibn 'Ali

---

[1] Transmitted by Al-Bukhari (110) and Muslim (2134), on the authority of Abu Huraira ⚜.

111

was by his side. The Prophet was looking once at the people and once at Al-Hasan ibn 'Ali saying, "This son of mine is a Sayid (i.e. a noble) and may Allah make peace between two big groups of Muslims through him"."[1]

All sorts of benefits from lineage and relations would cease on the Day of Resurrection except the lineage and relations of the Prophet ﷺ; Allah ﷻ said: ﴾And when the Trumpet is blown, there will be no kinship between them that Day, nor will they be able to ask one another﴿[2]. Imam Ahmad reported a Hadith on the authority of Al-Miswar, who said: "The Prophet ﷺ said: "Fatima is a part of my body; what hurts her hurts me and what pleases her pleases me, and all kinship will cease on the Day of Resurrection except my kinship and lineage".[1] This Hadith is in the two Sahih books[2] on the authority of Al-Miswar with a different narration.

Omar ibn Al-Khattab ؓ said that when he asked to marry Um Kalthum, daughter of Ali ibn Abu Talib ؓ, Ali said to him: "She is young", Omar ؓ said: "I heard the Messenger of Allah saying: "all kinship will cease on the Day of Resurrection except my kinship and

---

[1] Transmitted by Al-Bukhari (2704), Abu Dawud (4662) and Attirmidi (3773), on the authority of Abu Bikra ؓ.
[2] Surah Al-Mu'minun, verse 102.
[1] A sound Hadith, transmitted by Ahmad (323/4) and Al-Hakim (158/3), on the authority of Al-Miswar ibn Makhrama ؓ. It was also mentioned by Sheikh Al-Albani in Sahih Al-Jami' (4189).
[2] Transmitted by Al-Bukhari (3714) and Muslim (2449), on the authority of Al-Miswar.

lineage"[3], so I would dearly love to have kinship with the Messenger of Allah ﷺ. Ali ؓ agreed and married his daughter to Omar ؓ.

The scholars said that the Muslim Ummah is related to the Prophet ﷺ on the Day of Resurrection, and that the nations of other prophets are not related to them. However, it was said that it is beneficial for the Muslim Ummah to be related to the Prophet ﷺ, and it is not the case for other nations with their prophets. Allah ﷻ said: ﴿And remember the Day when We shall raise up from every nation a witness against them from amongst themselves﴾[1] and He ﷻ said: ﴿And for every Ummah, there is a Messenger; when their Messenger comes, the matter will be judged between them with justice, and they will not be wronged﴾[2]. These are among many verses, which show that each Ummah will be called on the Day of Resurrection with the Prophet who was sent to them. And Allah ﷻ knows best.

---

[3] A Sound hadith, transmitted by Attabarani in Al-Kabir (2633) Al-Hakim (142/3) and Al-Baihaqi (7/64, 114), on the authority of Omar ibn Al-Khattab ؓ.
[1] Surah An-Nahl, verse 89.
[2] Surah Yunus, verse 47.

*Al-Firdous Limited Presents, for the first time
in the English language*

Tafsir Ibn Kathir

*Abridged by Sheikh Muhammad Nasib Ar-
Rifa'i*

An abridged version of the most famous
collection of Tafsir (Explanation of the Qur'an)
by al-Hafiz Abul Fida Ismail Ibn Kathir (701
AH) translated into the English language. This
Tafsir needs no introduction. It is one of a few
that deals with explaining the Qur'an by the
Qur'an, the Qur'an by the Sunnah and then by
the opinions of the predecessors. The original
tafsir is rather elaborate and like a manual for
scholars and students of knowledge. In this work,
Shaykh Rifa'i has managed to retain the original
meaning, the intricate details and the unique style
of the original work. A long overdue translation

of a classical tafsir. An essential reading for the serious students.

The Al-Firdous publication of Ibn Kathir's tafsir is unique because:

1. Sheikh Muhammad Nasib Ar-Rifa'i has taken out completely the Israeliate (stories from the Jewish sources) from his version of Ibn Kathir.

2. Every hadith has been classified in the footnotes by Sheikh Mukbil bin Hadi Al-Wadia

3. The Majority of the hadith are Sahih (correct) hadith.

4. There are endorsements by seventeen of the highest scholars in the word from various countries for the version by Shaykh Rifa'i which is why it has been chosen by Al-Firdous.

5. Sheikh Rifa'i's version of Ibn Kathir is accurate, preserving the character of the original.

DAJJAL
THE FALSE
MESSIAH

IMAM IBN KATHEER

THE RETURN OF

HIJAAB

PART I

عودة الحجاب

DR. MUHAMMED IBN AHMED IBN ISMAIL

THE RETURN OF

HIJAAB

PART II

DR. MUHAMMED IBN AHMED IBN ISMAIL

THE RETURN OF

HIJAAB

PART III

عودة الحجاب

DR. MUHAMMED IBN AHMED IBN ISMAIL

TAFSĪR
IBN KATHĪR

PART 9

Sūrah Al-A'raaf, ayat 88 to 206
Sūrah Al-Anfal, ayat 1 to 40

ABRIDGED BY
Sheikh Muḥammād Nasīb Ar-Rafā'ī

Al-Firdous Ltd., London